novum pro

AF009983

Badiaa Hiresh

Where is
My Angel?

novum pro

www.novum-publishing.co.uk

All rights of distribution, including film, radio, television, photomechanical reproduction, sound carrier, electronic media and reprint in extracts, are reserved.

Printed in the European Union, using environmentally-friendly, chlorine-free and acid-free paper.

© 2015 novum publishing

ISBN 978-3-99048-184-4
Editor: Louise Darvid
Cover photo:
Haywiremedia | Dreamstime.com
Cover design, layout & typesetting: novum publishing

www.novum-publishing.co.uk

The journey started with agony, screams and pain; that is all I heard and felt.

Hey, is someone there? I asked. Where is everybody? Where did you all go?

Is that how we receive a newborn? I was told I will be cherished! I was told I will find a group of people around me, ready for me, expecting me! I was told I will be someone's daughter, brother, sister, cousin! This means lots of people out there! I was told I will be treated like an angel! But instead, this weird reception! Why is everyone looking at me this way? Why are some of you ignoring me and avoiding eye contact? Where is the lady that was supposed to hug me when she first sees me? I was told she will be my mommy, and kids have only one mommy! Hey, Mommy, are you there?

… that was the answer! Silence was the answer!

Can someone tell me what is happening? Well, it's after a long while that a white coat with glasses came to me. Oh I know, this is the angel that promised me all the beautiful things. The white coat said, Dear Child, I'm sorry to tell you, what a beginning! Fate knocked at the door of your mommy, and she traded places with you. You are now on your own. Stay strong!

But wait, you are not the angel that promised me a beautiful life, where are you, my angel?

My angel was just there, in the corner, looking at me with silence and never left!

That is how my journey started, with agony, screams and pain … It was day one that I learned that pain is relative to the mind, and if we are not strong enough to stand alone, pain will overpower us! But remember I was only a child back then …

I dedicate this book to inner-strength, to women in general and remember that beauty is inside you; to my mother on the death bed and your thoughts at that moment; to my daughters: because of you I am who I am today; to me and here is what I have learned so far ...

I am not looking for empathy, I am not looking for tears, I am not asking you to learn from my mistakes although not all are mistakes, I just wish you get to learn with time about the package that made me the person I am today.

Chapter 1

December 6 1964, the day launched with fatal news. The loss of a beautiful 26-year-old woman. Yes, I was the black sheep, at least in my own eyes. I was the newborn that morning, the reason behind the loss of that beautiful young lady, my birth-mother. She was beautiful, with a strong personality, charisma, charm, and mainly she was the mother of two boys; four and two and a half and a six and a half year old girl. It was a tragedy in the family. It is the unfairness of life, we can call it fate, destiny, or a call; I just call it "things happen for a reason," but till now I did not find the reason.

Living without a mother is tough. A mother is the source of strength, comfort, love; a mother is the guidance to perfection; a mother is the devil's advocate; a mother is the cover up of mistakes; a mother is the cook, the driver; a mother is the beginning. She gives her child everything, knowing that her child owes nothing in return. That is what I lost, and I'm still trying to know why! But unfortunately, no one wants to discuss it, or there is no one out there to discuss it with.

The loss of my mother was devastating to my father. He truly was lost. He tried his best to take care of the family, but being a man, he dealt with things as a man would. Same with my grandmother, losing the first born is a tragedy on its own, in addition to the fact that her child was the mother of four children … I don't know how I would react; all I know is definitely I cannot judge any of them for whatever happened but as for blame, I will let you and time decide.

People mourn in different ways, regenerate their strength through different means, and some move back in the original direction, while others wander towards the unknown. This is human nature. When we reach the point of fragmentation in life, the only possible way to move on is through accepting the situation, collecting the pieces, connecting them together, and moving on. At times, mourning is not the answer, especially when you have little souls depending on us. I respect everyone's pain, but life goes on.

At the beginning, we lived side by side by my grandparents' house, my mother's side. As I heard, my father had nannies taking care of the house and the four kids. My grandparents were there, but I don't know how much and I don't know why slowly they disappeared out of our life. They were a big family, ten kids and my grandparents, till the loss of my mother. With time they all vanished, as many things and people did throughout.

To me and until I became at an age where memories can be stored, things were vague.

I recall the beating by the nanny as a toddler with the wooden washing stick. I do not know the reason but regardless nothing justifies it. I recall my dad following her on the street to beat her up, after he saw the bruises on my face and body. Do I recall that; I don't know, probably this is a factual story I was told! But I still feel the pain inside me and mainly the scars are still there under my eye and by my eyebrow to this day. Truth is, the pain inside is deeper than the scars. It's a pain shadowed by fear, that still walks down the road till today without knowing its source.

The fear and pain created a fighter. A fighter that escaped battles and chose different ways to stand alone. I don't know if I can call myself a fighter, since fighters need back up, a battlefield and strategies. The back up component has never been there, the battlefield is my path while strategies, I don't know if I had time to create, since all the way from birth till today, my life has been a roller coaster.

We had two houses, my memory tells me. The summer house in the mountains and another one in the city for the fall season. At age eight, my dad remarried. I and my brethren attended the wedding. My father was fifty back then. My step-mother was a divorcee of twenty-two years old whom my father helped through the divorce.

The situation of our family required a radical change, and my father had the right to move on. The mother-to-be was a beautiful woman, young enough to have sufficient energy for the new step-children, experienced as a mother because of a son she had already, ready to take over an open position in a broken home, and eager to build a family. The perfect bride for the perfect situation, but of course, with her own story ...

The mountain house, I loved. It was there where I had great memories: tree climbing, bicycle rides and of course my first kiss by age ten. I was the tom boy of the village, growing up among boys played a huge role. I was the only little girl on the tree with a dress. My father really spoiled us in terms of clothing and needs. He did the impossible to make us feel happy. As for being close to him, I always felt there was something standing there. Was it the loss of my mother? Was it the concern of raising four children? Or was it how much he knows about children? Between conflicts of knowhow, sorrow and love, he was always there within distance.

At age ten, my half-sister was born. A beautiful baby with beautiful green eyes, who became the dolly of the house. She became everyone's focus and center of attention. I had mixed feelings about her. I don't know if it was related to the fact that finally, once I had a mother, I had to share her again with a newborn. I was the first among my brethren to call my step-mother "mommy". It was easier to me than to my brethren due to the fact that I never met my mom and mainly I was longing for a motherly love. School has never been easy, kids talking about their mothers, mother's day, and festivities ... my parents' seats were always empty. I tried with time to build a defensive shield that protected me from pain but emptiness was growing as well.

The first years of honeymoon started fading away, my older sister could not adapt to the presence of the new mother, which created conflicts in the house. One morning I woke up to a set of memories torn, the pictures of my mother and us at young age, pictures belonging to the phase before my dad's remarriage. It aggravated my sister more than others. After a while she left home and went to my grandparents' home, where conflicts arose as well. So she moved from one uncle's house to the other where she finally settled in the house of the priest, a family friend, in the States. My sister was attached to serving the church since I remember. I don't know if things would have been different if my dad had not remarried, but how would I know. Facts are, he did remarry, and my sister had to leave the house seeking her own happiness. Here goes another family member, from inside my house, and who knows what is best? Her news with time started decreasing, and we went on to a different struggle. It is sad, still till this day, I wonder why do people fight, why is it that my sister did not adjust and cope with the new family set up? Why is it that members in this unit did not fight to keep the family together? But sadly, no one can give answers. Is it fate? Is it what is best? Who knows! I learned to accept what is happening around me, I learned to strengthen the shield and use it to protect me from my pain.

During this time my grandparents became a distant family, I recall spending a Christmas dinner with them. But distance became deeper and I started feeling like a stranger. My bedroom, in which I shared my sister's difficulties, had an empty bed. Nightmares shadowed me during the lonely nights, and unanswered questions during the days. All I learned; life goes on.

Adjusting to a family routine was a struggle. A happiness that missed some pure factors was growing as well. Some beautiful moments made me closer to my step-mother. But there was always fear of the upcoming. After a phase of wilderness, we had to follow rules and create new memories. It was easy and hard at the same time. Yet we survived as a family, I started growing; learning to be a mother. My mind was recording all the moments and facts. As for my heart, it was holding back because I learned that what is meant to happen is stronger than all power. Somewhere along the way I lost something precious. Happiness has a price!

In 1974, the thirty years civil war started in Lebanon. By then, we had moved from our house by my grandparents to another house in the city. We were still going to the mountain house, but with the war situation, we had to leave both houses and move to the Christian area of town. Farewell to memories, school friends, and neighborhood. It was a beautiful house, where new memories started building up. But when fate calls, we just respond. After my sister left, the Sunday church visit disappeared. I did not know what to pray for or how to pray, I started losing the habit and sticking to the prayers taught at school.

After a while and because of the war, both my brothers left for Germany. My older brother was less than fourteen. They started visiting. It was tough losing them as well. But life goes on.

With or without them, I lived on my own, surrounded by memories I wanted to erase, others I created. Life was not easy, but the fighter inside me, the fighter without soldiers, emanated with a shield strong enough to survive.

Chapter 2

As I was growing, I always saw the same nightmare. A snail swelling and extending its shell to block my way every time I wanted to pass. This dream lived with me for years. I was young, I couldn't do anything about it, and it just added fear to my heart. Till today, I live with the fear of darkness on top of all other fears. With time I learned to isolate my fears and move on. But I never knew, that through isolating my fears, I started locking loads of emotions that made me the woman I am today. Sometimes I feel I can defeat any situation, sometimes I feel I can change situations, and other times I just want to hide and let go. Truly, I did defeat, change and manage a lot but till today I did not hide; more importantly, till today, I did not face. I believe it is related to the fact that I always felt alone among the group of people surrounding me. It goes back to day one, the day I discovered the power protecting me, NONE!

Women are the reflection of the home they came from and the society they lived in. I was raised in a way to conquer the picture not the content. Good or not, probably time shall decide! I cannot go back in time and change things, as I cannot decide for others. Although people in general are in charge of their reaction to different situations, age plays a big role. If you ask me today what would you have changed … well, I don't have an answer yet!

Since I was a teenager, my thoughts about the future were to become an independent and successful business woman who would live abroad, single with thirteen children; while other kids wanted to be a mommy, a ballerina or a teacher. I was a rebel, those were the days of the seventies. My thoughts for the future were to break through. I used all the pain, fear and loneliness I lived to dream about freedom, creating my own world, and mainly away from the people who were in my life. Intentionally or not, new circumstances arose, giving me more determination to break through. And here I was, living my teenage years, with deeper emotions locked. During this phase, more space stood between me and God, with more questions to … why me?!

Despite all, I was the happy go lucky girl! Yes, I was. But what the people around me did not know, was that every day that went by, I had deeper scars instilled in me.

Home during that phase consisted of my father, my step-mother and my step-sister. My sister's news was almost fully vanished, her mentioning at home had zero existence but in my heart she kept a scar that always had one question, why was she gone? As for my brothers who were visiting during the holidays, it was a time of joy seeing them till …

The war took over most of the areas in our country except where we lived. My father managed to keep us protected and away from all danger. My step-mother's mother, brother and sisters used to come and stay over for days, view the safety factor where they lived. I bonded with my step-grandmother. Laughs and giggles throughout the nights, more than bonding with the kids. She was a mature and smart lady. During that phase, my step-mother and I started getting really close. Closer than I was to my dad. I cherished those days. But as I learned to keep distance from happiness, I was always hesitant. As for school, during this phase, I still was on top of my class, and was always exempt from the final exams. I believe those were some of the best days.

When you live in home having a father like mine, you will be envied for all you have. My father was a man full of life, a man who had a position in society, well-known, respectable, well-dressed and outgoing. His personality filtered down towards his family. I recall the days under his roof, under his wings, we were well-known in the society. He loved life, he embraced it. I still hear his giggles watching TV … I still remember the smell of his perfume … Life with him was full of life … It is said when a daughter has it all under her dad's wings, she can conquer the world! Indeed it is the only true statement! And again conquer the picture and not the content.

What I did not have, living with a dad like mine, was a boyfriend. My dad was from the old school, and I was in an all-girl school. So the boyfriend issue was a mystery to me till my rebel personality broke through. My brothers at this phase started coming often, and here is the time where things started changing.

Loving our kids is a very important matter, showing them respect is great and it starts at early age because it will give them inner-power to succeed, but giving your child a pair of shoes bigger than his shoe size will make him trip. I might be eight in shoe size, in that case I might be able to wear eight wide, long or eight and a half, and prove myself; but wearing a size nine shoe, given to me by my parents and not to other brethren will affect my steps in addition to abusing my energy. I believe that each child has different potential, parents are in charge of developing them and most importantly keeping the family together as long as possible. If I have a problematic child, I don't throw him away. Before punishing him, I should dig deep down to reach the roots of his problems. That is the right thing to do.

But what has happened for people to vanish away from my life? Yes I ask again; I asked yesterday, today and I will ask every day. My human nature will tell you that my sister had difficulty coping with a new mom; my grandparents had difficulty coping with another woman replacing their daughter; my … etc.! I will give excuses to everything, and probably I will tell everyone what they need to hear. One of the survival steps I learned is being a pleaser to avoid problems. The truth is, I knew much more, there were factors that facilitated everyone's exit from my life; they were factors with a set agenda.

Slowly, and through different signs, things started getting cloudy in the house. Was it the house environment? Was it the number of people in the house? Was it the economic situation in the country? Was it the fact that my brothers were in and out of the country? Or was it the mist of unspoken words?

All I know it started getting darker!

It was around that time that I started feeling that I have a strong sense of empathy. My observing sense became even deeper. I grew eagle's eyes that penetrated walls and bionic ears that heard the unspoken. I don't know if it was a positive thing but I felt that I had the load of a fifty-year-old lady at age fourteen. I felt I was trying to solve everybody's problems, I felt their pain as well as I felt the twinkle in their eyes but worst, I knew the reason behind their feelings without discussing it.

This energy allowed me to expect things to happen, sadly! Yes sadly, because I went through the pain twice, the first time was to expect it, and the second time to deal with it.

I used to sit and wait, and then it comes! I will never wish any of my children living with that gift, not even any other child. This energy made me lose the innocence of my childhood, it abused my emotions; although I felt I grew faster and older than my age but I never developed the know-how or wisdom to deal with things back then. The only talent I developed with time was the talent of silence, feeling burying and emotion isolation, and all that with a smile on my face.

At that time, I did not know the importance of a proactive approach to things. Remember, I was in my early teens.

Children need time to grow, need to feel secure to build self-confidence, need reassurance to feel trust in self and others. We might shower them with gifts, food and clothing but nothing replaces the first years of support.

Children cope differently with different situations and that is where their personality plays its role, if they were treated equally. In addition to the factor of perception. Perception of a child to our actions is more important than our actions, as little as saying good morning to one and hello to the other.

Therefore, going back to my brothers and sister, each reacted differently to the family situation. I'm sure they have many questions related to all issues; as many as I have or probably more, but view that open communication among us had never been there, so I cannot speak for them.

How was I affected and what is different between me, my brothers and sister.

I believe, more or less, it started with the factor that I never knew my mom, that was to my advantage not theirs; what I went through with the nannies is a disadvantage to me; them living with both parental love even for the limited number of years they did, is an advantage for them. I call it the colostrum of life; losing a mom was a chocking truth that I have no doubt, it left a huge damage.

Advantages and disadvantages are countless, but counting was not the issue, it was not a race, instead it was a survival kit where we all had to build our own personalities away from all damage.

Around that time, my step-mother got pregnant again to have a beautiful baby boy whom I adored. This boy, was all to me; I helped raise him. I was so attached to both him and my baby sister. With time both of them gave me a weird feeling, I never knew how a mother would love but, I would say a motherly love. I danced with them, fed them, took them out … but him, view my age, fourteen years old, he filled a big emptiness in my life despite the mist of darkness that was covering the walls and ceiling of the house.

This mist grew a ghost, and the ghost started shadowing me. It started appearing to me. At times I felt it acted as my guardian angel but other times it created problems.

And at age fourteen, the problems were so painful that they affected my life on a personal, emotional and family level.

From that moment on, life became a rollercoaster. And all I wondered, will it ever take a rest?!

Chapter 3

In general, being a teenager is one of the difficult phases in life. Those who have everything rosy around them, will still go through growing pain. If I tell you I was never happy, I will be lying; I always managed to seek and reach happiness.

To me, those who are unhappy are those who allow darkness to overpower them. I am a happy person and I was blessed with this energy since I can remember. There are no standards that say you have to have x, y and z to be happy. It could be an issue of contentment to some of us, to others a materialistic issue, but only few are those who manage to reach an odd happiness.

Look around you, everyone has a smile on their face ... Not true!

Many forget to smile.

The first step towards happiness is to keep a smile on your face. Some people think that they are born with a heavy load; that they cannot be happy; that no one has the problems they have; that their life is a limited edition ... well, I think what makes our life a limited edition is the way we react to our situations and in simple terms what we make of our life. This does not mean do not be sensitive, compassionate, or empathetic, no, it just means give and take from others up to a level that it will not interfere with your own happiness. There is a big difference between a smile and a lively smile. You need to keep a lively smile on your face, not only will it attract positive vibes from the universe but, as well, it will project a positive character to others.

The lively smile comes from inside you, from your soul; it takes time and effort to reach that deep. You have to dig inside your soul, go through every layer, peel them one by one, accept them as parts of your life and go on. Acceptance plays a major role in our life. Once we stop dwelling on the roots, the tree will flourish. And so is our life, we don't need to cure every disease.

Some people live with their diseases throughout their life, they just learn to move on. So, unfold your soul, drag your puzzle behind by choice because if I suggest you drop it, it might hold you back. Drag it lightly, move on, carry that smile that shows who is the master of the game.

The second step towards happiness is to find a reason to be happy and do something that makes you happy. It may not be easy, but it has to be unique to you and convenient to your situation.

The phase I lived between ages fourteen and seventeen was not a ferry boat ride. Yet, I managed to be happy. It was a phase where I tried to keep a simple smile; it was a phase where my focus was to prevent my mind from wandering; it was a phase where I tried to teach myself the law of survival! I had to make a choice as a minor, a choice to stay or go, while what I failed to maintain was internal peace and sanity. The load was way heavier than my potential. Too many ghosts walking me through, a suction tunnel pulling all happiness syndromes from the house like a vampire and gossip here and there growing on every wall like grape leaves. So I started thinking about the healing process, and getting the internal pain out. I wanted to keep my focus from being attracted towards my surroundings as it drained all my mental and physical power. One important factor was that the main characters that stood in the way of happiness were mostly always around and in action. So I started taking notes, and notes turned into a diary, and then I started painting. I spent hours finding myself, I lost all interest in academics and I started losing contact with my surroundings. This was one of the laws of survival, isolate the pain, and then allocate a priority. The priority at that time was my sanity, so I tried to create a firewall standing between me on the inside and me on the outside. I was too young to understand and put a long-term goal, yet I was happy. I was able to seek refuge on paper. My short-term goal was to develop my inside while protecting it and not letting it sink. It was not easy, pain like happiness connects senses, and as it can create flourishing times, it can lead to breakdowns of the systems.

Soon after, I started developing stress health symptoms, stomach pain, jaw pain, headaches and dizziness … I told myself back then, "Finally, I got saved by a holy power, and here he is sending his angels to pull me back." The pain was unbearable, followed by insomnia; but it was not time to go!

There were no medical explanations for my pain but stress, yes at that age. It is not easy to ask a teenager to understand pain that is not medically diagnosed and or justified. When doctors were crossing off all medical possibilities, I just wanted to ask them whether they believed in ghosts. I needed someone to know, I needed to share my thoughts, my feelings … but who would believe it? Would I be facing another dilemma, other than the ghosts? That was my concern.

Suddenly I started hearing echoes and gossip about me; I looked around and asked myself whether it was true. I started doubting myself. Do I sleep walk? Do I have a double personality? I was so certain of being innocent from all accused of. I was certain from catching the ghost in action at four o'clock in the morning destroying the family. I was certain that I was in pain. But who would believe a fourteen-year-old girl? Can a fourteen-year-old girl stand against the world?!

And here was another reason pushing me to be stronger. It was me against the ghosts and the world.

All I wanted was to end either the reality or the dream I was living through. All I desired was to be a teenager, to live a normal life, to be simply happy.

I did not want to live the odd happiness, yet I had no choice. Sadly at a very young age, I had to have an odd life. I had to choose to either take it or leave it.

Since I believed that happiness comes from within, that happiness is a state of mind and people must reach inner-peace before seeking happiness, so I went again, conquering the inside of my soul to seek inner-peace.

The third step towards happiness is to find a comfort zone that is made of humans and things. It is the most difficult step since trust in humans is the main factor. Anything related to materials can increase and decrease, exist and disappear. We can build it and leave, once we come back it will always be here. We can be attached to it, yet no hard feelings. Therefore, the comfort zone part focusing on things is easy to handle, build and find. The dilemma exists when it comes to the comfort zone focusing on humans. I believe people are born with a natural sense of trust towards others. With time and through experiences, it will develop. Age and maturity play a significant role in finding it. But since anything related to humans is unpredictable, so is trust. If I want to discuss my own experience, it took me a while to accept that my birth mom did not choose to leave me. My first thoughts were that she betrayed me, she let go, she did not hold on to life and especially me. Was it a fact? Of course not, but come discuss it with a toddler looking around and finding mothers cherishing their kids; discuss it with a child looking around and hearing mothers tucking in their children, kissing them good night, reading a bed time story and preparing their favorite snacks; discuss it with a teenager looking around and seeing others worrying about their hairstyle, clothing and normal teenage issues while in my case, trust was a swing that was taking me from one side to the other. I had to analyze, accept, fold and smile in order to find trust. Till one day, early in life, I was in my last teen years, I asked myself the magical question. Why is it that my heart was on hold, my mind tells me something and my actions do something else? Well the answer was very simple; I started living a pretend game. Some out there will be offended if I did not show trust, others, trusting them was a given, and last were those I trusted, given the trust till further notice. Along the way, I started learning that pretend trust is the game I have been watching and everyone uses others to fit their own agenda.

    Around that time, both my older brothers moved back almost permanently, and I restored my solidarity with my older brother. Both my older and oldest brothers joined my dad's work. It was a beautiful picture. While each having their own character and style, they managed to make the best out of things. When you are not on the other side of the frame, you see what your eyes show you. I either saw a beautiful picture or saw what I wished to have, the family back together.

Days passed, weeks and months, I was able to feel the colors of the family picture fading away; I was able to sense tension growing. Words were decreasing in the house and among its occupants ... I became a stranger and at times I wished I was. I could not handle the pain any more. Why was there black and white colors only? Where are the gray shades? How can people have two faces? Why is there hatred? Why is there rage and anger? I started wondering whether people will vanish again.

All signs were poor, and projecting negativity. It was like fog coming down slowly, covering the brightness of the day, and diminishing visibility. Why is happiness so hard to reach, why is happiness not meant to be, were we destined to live loneliness while living in a community full of people? The ghosts started twisting the winds in the house, and like tornadoes the view was impossible, all I heard was that another family member vanished with the storm. Who was it? I was worried, scared, trying to guess or setting preferences ... I couldn't, each was special in their own way!

So I went to my diary, the diary that was my refuge. I put my thoughts and described the situations. Sadly, I did not receive an answer. Of course not, the diary was my refuge and the refuge is just a temporary place till we seek solutions.

I left the world of reality to create my own real world. Indeed, at times, the diary spoke to me; through my words I saw the pain, and between the lines I started seeing the rainbows. Day after day, the diary had it all. It carried the story, and between the lines, it carried hope. It could not heal my wounds, but definitely showed me the way to Faith, Hope and better days. The diary that was my refuge and through its lines I found my salvation, became my hurdle. The ghosts knew about it and feared it would destroy them. They shook the house and agitated its occupants until I was cornered by black eyes and fingers pointing at me. I was forced to destroy it. Bye bye diary, you served your days. You knew it all. You helped me stand strong. Sadly I have to destroy you, me, the only person you gave hope to ... I know you understand.

Indeed, the diary answered by saying, "They can destroy words but never erase the story that made me the person I am today, the rest will be written on invisible pages, and destiny shall reveal the truth one day!"

Chapter 4

It was like a dream, another wake up call, and a call that shook my present, past and brought up the painful memories I was trying to ignore and forget.

I was in my room, supposed to be sleeping, it was around two a.m. I heard a noise in the house. It was creepy, but fear cannot be scary when expected. Although the noise was growing bigger and bigger no one heard a thing. Only I could hear it, indeed I did. And I heard it not because it was noisy but because I was waiting for this moment to come. Then, suddenly, and for no reason I saw myself sitting in bed, waiting for the door to open. Around that time, I heard footsteps coming closer. I opened the door, he was standing there. No, it was not a ghost, it was my older brother. I looked around, all his clothes were packed. I could not say much, I had more tears inside my heart than rolling down my cheeks. These few minutes lasted longer than hours, I did not know what to do. Should I scream, call someone, ask for help? I knew not to! Instead, I just tried to look at him one last time. He hugged me and said, the house is getting too crowded, the ceiling is dropping too low, I can't stay anymore; you should move on before you will not find a room for you.

Was it time? Will I ever see you again? Will you contact me? Those were my words, as for the answers, I did not expect any, and none were said.

And like a breath of air, he passed by to escape the crowd. One more down.

Why? My questions to the Higher Authority increased. I know the Lord does not plan painful paths, I know the Lord gives us choices, I know the Lord gives us hope and mainly I know to keep faith in my heart. But wait, again and again why do I have to know and expect and understand. So I decided to shuffle my thoughts. Rebel was the answer, and it was the feeling inside me. Against whom? was my question ... No one! My blood was no longer just flowing inside my veins, it was rather boiling throughout my heart, soul and brain. Tell me black, I smile and say yes; tell me night, I close my eyes and wonder why you suggest that; tell me eat, I wonder if it is poisonous, fattening or not tasteful! I used to look at myself in the mirror and say, no, it was not me. That is how far trust was gone, yet with a smile.

Around that time, I started university. I went to college, decided on a major, it was journalism. I got the application home, and the next day it vanished. I switched ... within minutes to plan B. Simple? Very! Not a true statement. The true statement was "I Don't care!" As well not a totally true statement. The very true statement was ... I am my own world, but not in an egocentric way. My focus was to build my life, fake on the outside while protecting the inside. So I started with a smile. I promised myself that no one is allowed to access my firewall. Day after day, I tried to heal the wounds ...

I could not. So plan B was, SKIP (Seal-Keep-Isolate-Pretend).

Seal the wounds untreated, Keep memories in mind but Isolate the related emotions and last Pretend you are ignorant, you are happy, you are fine. Bottom line, I understood that I am in charge of my own life, happiness and well-being. I understood as well, that people don't care if they hurt others especially if they need to protect themselves; and mainly I understood that people don't like negative and depressed attitudes regardless of how much in pain and/or close we are.

So I switched to plan B. I did not care about what's taken away, I cherished what I had. I protected myself through SKIP in a way where I felt emotionally impenetrable. It was tough, but it was the only way to put the past on hold. And so be it, within different plans here and there, I ended up working at my dad's retail business. It was a nice change, challenging new beginning but mainly, it was there where I met my first love. I wouldn't call it love since my emotions were mixed up or rather messed up; but yet yes, it was the first time I experienced that feeling. A feeling of strength, attraction, butterflies, flirts, etc. ... and better yet a feeling of who is the man! Not a nice statement, but in other words, who is in charge!

Through working at my dad's place, I started meeting new people, interacting, creating, being held responsible for different things ... I found myself away from all stress and ghosts, in other words I found myself. I was afraid to show happiness, as I was afraid it would be taken away. Soon after I started meeting more people, making new friends within the frame possible; if you remember, my dad was from the old school and I had to respect the frame he built us.

What I noticed around that time, is that I developed a new characteristic, the "low expectation," in my own words and definitions at least.

My main concern was to build myself a shrine. It might be a huge word but the idea behind it was huge. Inside that shrine, we will have many people coming and leaving at their convenience, tied by friendship and unexpected to stay.

I made myself new goals that I carried away with a smile. I had to create a focus that would help me secure my peace of mind and sanity. I can't live in the past, I can't ignore the past, the past made my present and I have to live my life. So my second goal was to wear a mask that would present a barrier between my emotions and the expressions on my face. But one thing I failed to hide, the look in my eyes.

So I pushed myself towards the unknown, towards living a new adventure. I had no fear, instead I had a craving to live by the edge. No rules were my rules ... be happy and live your life!

It turned out I was not alone ... more people joined the shrine, with smiles and tears from strangers, I formed a caring family.

My brother was gone, and instead of one family member that was my sister, I had two members, my brother and my sister that I kept trying to track and worry about. But when you have friends like mine and a sister-in-law like my brother's wife, they all helped remain in touch with my brother and updated me on his news. As for my sister, news was almost far away gone.

Meanwhile, I got more attached to this guy I met at work. A pure, so called friendly relation that gave me hope and ongoing feeling for a good future. Years passed, the war in the country was still ongoing. My father tried opening new businesses in the neighboring countries. I used to travel with him.

Between my presence with him at work, and travelling with him, I finally got close to him. A new bonding formed, and truly, I got to know my father and got very close to him. I was sorry for the days I missed, because truly he was a great man and father.

I guess, the Holy power from above was around, feeling and seeing the pain. It turned out I was not alone seeing the ghosts. My father did as well. So he started sharing his side of the dilemma. I did not know which one was worst, mine or his. All I know, each perceived their presence in a different way. The good part, even if I was to ignore my feelings and story, I got to be close to my father, and ease his pain by being near him and listening to him. All I know, the good part, he did not know about the pain the ghosts had caused me. I couldn't add any pain to his by sharing my own dilemma. By then I had just learned that my feelings were true, the ghosts existed and I was not alone. All I know that there was a Holy power. Would things get better? I never had an answer. That was way far, there were no signs.

The shrine had more visitors with whom I connected. Regardless of the ghosts, low ceiling and fog inside the house, I managed to see a good time. Still I was very hurt from the loss of my brother, yet I was finding positive refuge with the guy I met at work. Till one day, he came to me, saying he would be travelling to the States. For good I said? The answer was no, but I have to finalize a family situation and when I come back, I will be coming back to you. My heart was jumping from joy. I looked up, to the Holy power, and thanked him for the signs of change. Two nights after, it was news time. I was at home in my room. I heard my dad saying, what a disaster, a plane just crashed in Lockerby. I froze, my tears started falling, I knew he was on that plane. The next day, I went to work, and we were officially informed of his presence on the plane. Farewell, dearest friend; I cried him for nights. Two weeks after, his friend came over with the memory book. He came to pay his condolences to me, telling me about how much hope and love his long gone friend had for me, and about his future plans with me. But what is not meant to be, shall never happen. So I wrote, "You will always have a special place in my heart! You will be missed!" I couldn't say more, it was too painful!

And back to my shrine I went, but this time I was convinced that there was something standing between me and the unknown, it was mysterious.

I went back to my shrine with the intentions to bury myself or rather my soul. Mainly not because I was sad, but because I started feeling that I was the carrier of a black aura ...

A decision was made! Stand up! Stand up for me before others ... When in life we start thinking or feeling that we are not living, alive or existing ... trust me it is scary. And when we start thinking that we might be a magnet to a negative sequence of events ... trust me it is bad. So I decided, if I am causing all the pain, I can be the healer. And irrelevant of facts, and who caused what, I believed that being the healer, I should start with own my soul.

So I embarked on a new spiritual journey ... still in my teen years. I decided that the soul has no age. The pain is relative to the heart, mind and body. So I became the healer, and I started with my soul.

First, it was the will part ... I want to exist.
Second, it was the "I do" part ... I want to heal.
Third, it was the "I can" part ... I can do it.
Fourth, it was the self-centric part ... I will do it alone.

I believed, at that age, that the power of the universe could not stand by me;

I believed that there were facts stronger than I am to handle;

And I believed that the ghosts were right on their mission and they will not let go till their mission is accomplished.

So, I started my own journey, on my own terms and conditions. I set the past aside with all its memories and pain. I started the healing process.

People were gone, others came along, and the war reached our area. My step-mother, both younger brother and sister, and my oldest brother left the country for a safe destination. Both brother and sister were enrolled in a school abroad. I had never lived the stress of the war till that time. Bombs reached our area, it was scary. I thought me and my father were going to die. We were alone, the rest of the family were gone. Some days I used to go with my dad to work, others when the situation was unstable, I used to stay at home.

I was really lonely, alone, scared and feeling beautiful. So I fell in love. Deep love that rejuvenated my life, soul, etc. ... it made me forget the war and wish it would last longer so the family abroad does not come back. The days were worth the years of my life that I totally forgot about. It was love!

A while after, the thirty years civil war ended, along with the dream I was living. The family came back, then again, again and again, the ghosts revealed a new story ... I shall never trust or love again!

Chapter 5

What's meant to be, shall be! True or not, to me it was.

For years, at night, I used to go to the private beach my family and I were members in. I used to sit there on the rocks overlooking the ocean, write poetry, letters to my brother that left, and throw my thoughts in the ocean. The ocean was my way out, my soulmate, where I released all my feelings. I could not start another diary, I could not live that deception again, so I let my feelings go and the ocean waves carried my thoughts in a bottle, towards the unknown.

Those days to me were only about love. You ask me about the weather, I answer about love, you ask about food, I think about love, you ask me about the war, sadness, people dying, and I feel the love. Love was in the air and I was living for love and living to love. I guess all the pain, agony and stress inside me were transformed into me loving others and being loved.

Did I live the love days of my life? I don't know. Did I go too far? Yes I did.

Did I hurt anyone? Never.

We met in the elevator. He was tall, handsome, green eyes, and with dark skin. He was Lebanese and worked for an international organization. Being me, I invited him for coffee. I didn't and still do not believe that only men take the first step. So here was a cup of coffee that never ended. I used to peek through the window, waiting for him to come, jump down to the lower level, in order to accidently take the elevator with him. One cup of coffee led to another, to lunch, to staircase meetings, on and on and on.

Did you ever experience love? Did you ever have a little sign that says I'm thinking about you? Did you ever have someone playing your song under your bedroom window? Did you ever have someone waiting on you all night? Did you ever have someone willing to take the extra mile for you? Did you ever have someone being the wise person while you offer all it takes?

Well, it was love, it was my story, and I know love was mutual. I do not believe it was temporary or situational. Did the safety circumstances and the war pressure intensify our emotions? It sure did but this does not mean that the emotions did not exist. When we, as women, feel that we are breathing because of him, want to wake up for him, want to do this or that for him, at this point I call it passion.

And this is true, I was passionately in love and I know he was too. The little secret life I lived was due to give me energy, the will to continue, and hope for the future, etc. I enjoyed it. I did not ask the questions I was supposed to ask; nor was I questioned. Back then, I did not know that when people don't ask questions, it means it is reciprocal. I thought we had no past to exchange, and I preferred not discussing my past. It was buried too deep to excavate. My main focus was living the day. I did not even discuss the future, ask or wonder about it. I wanted to live the moment, feel the joy, the lust, the love. Indeed, life was beautiful, people looking at me would see a woman in love, and I was.

Days passed, I woke up one day to unpleasant news, sadly this is how I felt, the war ended, it did. We received a call that the family was coming back from abroad. At the same time, I received a call from my so called man I loved, that he is going to the airport to pick up his family, then on a mission. The short conversation was clear and stated that we will not be able to talk for a while. I assumed that his family were his brothers and sisters, to my surprise … as I knew after, he was picking up his pregnant wife and daughter. The news burnt a part of my heart, what was left of my heart at least. In a second, I had to be strong, there was no place in my life for tears. My ego was too inflated to care about what people think, I had found love, but what did others find?

That phase like any other was costly. What was the cost? It was not clear yet. Within days, the gossip that was a whisper became an open out loud conversation. My story was the hit of the town ... all I had to say, silently, was anyone thinking or caring about my feelings?! Obviously not.

I could not be sad, I had lots of love that safeguarded me. All I was thinking, are you serious, do you have a conscience, a heart, and do you know the meaning of love?

And because I knew that happiness had a price, I had to pay. Within a week, I knew the price, I was being deported to the States. Being involved with a married man in our community, and in any community is not acceptable. Yet, no one took into consideration that I never knew. The States had been my dream since I was young, I had never been there. LA, California, here I come. The packing started, I was told to pack it all. My luggage reminded me of the goodbye scenery of my brother. It was a one way trip. One day, in the evening, my dad came into my room, he sat on the bed with tons of tears shedding on his cheeks. He broke my heart, it took him minutes to spill his words. This eve broke my heart, I was going to miss him, and I knew he was as well. He looked at the luggage and said what kind of fifteen day trip required seven pieces of luggage? At that moment, I knew that he did not know of the plan and nor was he part of decision. Again, the ghosts played their game. And the plan to empty the house from its tenants was ongoing. I remembered the goodbye words of my brother, the house is too crowded, the ceiling is falling low, get yourself out before they ship you out. My dad lost the only person he opened up to, me, I was his confidante. But unfortunately, a decision was made, I had to leave.

The farewell to my friends was difficult, including the boyfriend of five years I left before my last love. This one, after five years of pure relationship, he could not make it to my birthday, claiming he was stuck in his village because of the war situation. It was an evening of around thirty family members and family friends gathering for my birthday in a restaurant in the area. To my surprise, he popped in, escorted by a girl, but not to join us, he never knew we were there. At least that is what he claimed. Was it true, or was it planned through the ghosts ...? Who cares.

Pain was the only constant, pain was shadowing me. What's another one dropping out; I got used to this routine.

The married man I fell in love with tried contacting me, to explain. I refused any contact with him. The farewell was painful yet I had faith in a good journey.

Farewell Lebanon, friends, home, family, tenants and memories. Along with the packing, I had a film of pictures that was never developed. I took it along, only because I believed that the past, the memories and daily incidents were what made me the person I was that day. The day of travel, I looked at the door of my house and decided to lock it with all its content, from tenants, to my dad, the ghosts, and the memories. I had to take the evening boat to Cyprus, and from there I took the plane to the States. It was 1989, I went on the boat, located my room, and went back on the deck. I stood there, hearing the departure siren of the boat, I looked at the land that hosted me since birth, looked at the rocks by the ocean that carried my feelings, and the lights of the houses … they winked at me from far … farewell all of you, I closed a chapter of my life, and I shall never return again.

The journey with no return was my plan, with tears and heartbreaks the boat sailed.

Was I happy or sad? I never knew! All I knew, I was heading away, to the unknown, to an unpredictable future. My tears, I could not stop. I started talking to myself, I was possessed by fear, yet, I looked at the ocean that carried my thoughts for years, the ocean gave me a sign of comfort, a soothing feeling that I read as a blessing. The land, houses, lights and people by the shore starting fading away, and at this moment I realized that I was on my own. I turned my back to the known and I faced the unknown!

That night, I could not sleep, I was anxious, worried but somehow, I started feeling the excitement of a new sunrise. In the early hours of the morning, we reached Cyprus. I took a cab to the hotel, my flight was the next day. It was the first time I flew alone, but for one reason or another, I started gaining my strength. I decided, I am not a failure, I am not alone, and regardless of all incidents in the past, there is a power from above that shadowed me every step of the way, and I was sure it would never leave me.

I took a little tour in Cyprus, then the next day I took the cab to the airport, then to London. London gave me a flashback to the friend I lost in the plane crash in Lockerby. Then, on my way to the States, I had a last flashback on my life. Whatever took place since day one, was part of me. It was then where I learned, sitting alone with my thoughts, that we cannot ignore what made us who we are today. I decided to remember the good times, and learn the best lessons out of every event. To be honest, I started feeling proud of myself. I was 24 years old, speaking five languages, no degree, but with a load of maturity and wisdom people would reach at 80 years old. Incidents of my life could break many souls if they face one of them, I faced them all. I used every incident as a stepping stone towards my future. I decided to keep my book open and reuse all incidents as learning experiences. I learned that despite the unfair beginning, I grew up to be a 24-year-old woman. I learned that despite the sad incidents, I was able to reach an odd happiness. I learned that despite the obstacles, I was able to walk tall. I learned that despite the people I lost out of my life, I was able to create a shrine where more friends gathered and showed gratitude. I learned that despite the game played by the ghosts, I was able to reach my dad's soul after all. I learned that despite the tears shed, I was able to maintain a smile coming deep from inside my soul. I learned that despite the fog and low ceiling of the house, I was able to break through and create a firewall that protected me. I learned that despite the college education, I was able to seek knowledge and skills in a profession where I succeeded. I learned that despite all my losses and painful memories, I was able to find love. I learned that despite all, I had a power from above that shadowed me. All the despites made me a strong woman, unbeatable and mainly I was proud of the person I became.

Hours after, I reached the Promised Land. All along, since my early age, I dreamt of living single in LA. I told myself, welcome to my journey, I promise you I will never fail, I promise you that the woman who knocked your door today shall reach her potential.

I had to stay at a friend's house for a while until I found my own apartment. I had a job secured for me in Beverly Hills 90210. It was the jewelry shop of my family. I started looking for a place for me, I started work directly. I was happy, ready to conquer a new world, a new beginning.

One morning, at breakfast, the whole family was gathered, I heard a comment saying that I was a thief of married men. I stopped eating, packed my clothes and left the house with the decision to find my own place that day.

The ghosts were still active. I felt like an outcast, it looked like the war had no end!

Chapter 6

I was not a thief … and never a thief of married men. I appreciate the institution of marriage, I know what it means to have a family, I know how it feels to have a family, a fake family, or a broken family. I was played, manipulated and paid for my situation. But what is the cost one must pay for their situations. Although I was shipped to the States, to my dream destiny, to what I call the Promised Land, yet I have to say, it was tough, it was an exile. If I did not carry a warrior inside me, I would have been crashed. It was tough moving to a new country, new culture, where I actually had no friends or social life. Yet I made the step, and I decided to succeed.

Shortly after, I moved to my new place, I furnished it, and called it my castle. It truly was, inside those walls, rested my soul.

I kept in touch with the family and friends in LA within distance. It was not a physical distance as much as it was a mental one. After that comment, I told myself, ghosts can carry news their way, but I will prove myself my way.

Conflicts aside, it was time to move on. I bought a plane ticket to visit the sister I had not seen for around fifteen years. Wow, it was tough. With tears, hugs and kisses, we embraced each other, as if time was never lost. It was just a term, we actually grew up in different worlds, with different ideas and cultures. We were actually strangers. We had no memories together to share, we had nothing in common. The idea of us getting together again and renewing our sisterhood was a haze. There was one reality, she became the woman, wife and mother, destiny made of her. Another shock for me. I went back home, but this time we remained in touch. The sister I once had, I would never lose again, and so we did.

Still, with excitement and joy, I started every day, till I was hit by a severe virus, called culture shock. Although I was where

I always wanted to be, but daily, at sunset, I used to look at the horizon, with tears in my eyes and send messages back home; hoping to receive one back.

I started missing my family, friends and home. My heart was aching, aching so much that I couldn't cure it. I started extra jobs after hours to keep myself busy, my heart was still aching. I was making great money, my heart was still aching. Nothing would cure me and heal my pain, and worst, one day, I was at work, I received a call from the family telling me how shocked they were and that my father was ashamed with my actions, additionally, never to call home again, till things were settled. My response was, those among you with no sins cast me with a stone, of course a statement from the bible, and of course I did not say it.

I am a warrior but not a fighter, and to me there is a difference. It was wrong and still wrong till today, those who do not speak up, will never be defended. Especially when we live in a world where bystanders stand right and left. I said nothing, but the pain that was breaking my heart became acute, and I became desperate for a way out. It is one thing to miss someone but being forced out, is something else. With a smile I used to start my busy days, forcing myself to move on, and reminding myself that I am a self-healer. I kept on sinking. Soon after, I found a message, showing me the path of forgetfulness. The message came in a bottle, I used to start reading it at the end of the day, but sadly never view its bottom. The person who was conquering the new journey with fierceness, started falling apart and behind and that person was me. My outside was glowing and shining, while my inside was deteriorating and torn into pieces across the continents. Despite all the pain, my heart never neared hatred. Instead I kept on waiting for the light to pop from the darkened alleys. Like thirsty lost ones in the desert seeing illusions of water, I was waiting for the day the rays glowed again from the dark corner to bring everyone back … my optimism was good and bad. Good because it gave me hope and bad because waiting made me sink even deeper. My feelings were extreme, and at times I could not control the heaps; both extremes were heavy, and a solution was due. Unfortunately I saw the message in a bottle, but fortunately, I had a good friend.

One day, he came to me and reminded me of myself, my strength, my want to be, and exist; indeed he was a great friend. He reminded me of the person he saw when he first met me, and sometimes we need to hear that. So, on my feet I stood again, closed the book of my life as is, and put it aside. I started a new page, one that I knew I would collate one day to continue the puzzle.

A blank page, a pen, me and destiny ... and I wrote, I am a woman, destined to succeed and I shall do!

At this phase, I started seeing life from a different perspective. I refused to just go with the flow, yet I was not a fighter; I refused to let others guide me, yet I needed that push. Usually, that push comes from a source of support and trust, and it was not available. So as you could see, I was alone. I started evaluating myself, and I was surprised with my achievements. So I decided to slowly build my path, I started mingling with the community, and forming a new life. I succeeded, I was part of a group of friends, we travelled together, made plans together, and supported each other. Most of them were male friends. For one reason or another, and being surrounded by a business world while growing, my comfort zone lay in the male environment. I am not denying my feminine side, or enjoying a male companionship, but on a friendly level, that is where I rested my case.

Accidently, one evening, on a ladies' night out, my friend and I decided to go dancing. That was the first time after months in LA that I did such a thing. With a decision not to get introduced to anyone, I ended up meeting my husband. Knowing this place usually hosted people from the Middle East among Europeans and Americans, and knowing I definitely had no intentions to come back to Lebanon, we had decided to dance the night out and end it there. But when destiny is decided, sarcasm would be the answer. Among the many people that were there, and the only night I decided to go out ladies only, I had to meet my future husband. Of course, he booked us a table, champagne and flowers ... who would not fall for that?! One thing led to another, and things got serious.

Suddenly, one day, at the shop, the phone rang. I took the call, hearing the voice calling my nickname, I froze.

As if we split yesterday, the man I loved and could never hate, it was him on the phone. Till today, I cannot say he had the audacity to say he moved his wife and kids to Canada, then came to LA to look for me. Am I so naïve or do I believe in pure love? Why would he follow me there? Why would he go through all that hassle for me? Why is it that I cannot hate? I'm sure you think I went and met him ... Yes, I froze when I heard his voice; Yes, I wanted to see him; I didn't know if I would slap him, but I sure was missing being in his arms ... so, I said, never call me again!

He tried further, but I wanted to stay strong, and never heard from him again. Despite all the words I wanted to tell him, I stayed strong; especially as this was not what I was expecting at the end of the tunnel, I wanted my family back, they were my priority.

Day after day, the light at the end of the tunnel was fading away, with it went the hope of getting together with my loved ones. At that time, the painful memories started popping out again, but this time, I was determined to start the self-healing process for good, knowing that I was at the edge of an outburst.

Ghosts, early morning chaos, farewell, losses, etc. ... I had enough, one after the other. I started discussing them with myself, out aloud in front of the mirror. Occasionally, I argued with myself and many times, the me in the mirror refused to look me in the eyes. I guess the message was, I failed myself before any other. Although I never blamed myself for any incident, I could never forgive myself for being a bystander and taking no action, at least towards myself. The first person who was subject to prosecution was me. I never stood for myself, I never stood up for others.

Was I wrong, was I young or was I afraid? And then, was I fearing the ghosts or was I fearing losing the ghosts?

One step after the other, I detached myself from the past, mostly. Some emotions were more damaging than others, so I let time be.

Around that time, the recession in LA was just starting, a decision was made to close up the jewelry business. I tried looking around for another job, between my character not fitting in and getting closer to the person who became my husband, finding a new job did not take place. He did not encourage me to work for strangers and to be honest, I never thought I could do it. Shortly after, I was jobless, and married. Yes, within three months of the day we met. Here, I got to be introduced to a new me. I did love the man I met that night on the ladies' night out, the man who became my husband, in three months. Why did I marry so fast, why did I drop all my thoughts and dreams, why did I jump into the unknown? I was a risk taker, he was a gentleman, and it was an adventure. Among all the dreams I used to build in my head, one of them was to build a future from scratch with a gentleman. Separating love from passion, to me, journeys should not be planned carefully. I always believed that while putting the plan into action, time is wasted on thinking. I was young, wild, and risk free. The most successful moments in life are those unplanned because they are built with courage on a risk free surface. So, I ended up with a husband.

I announce you husband and wife ... at that moment I realized that it was no longer a dream. On my application there was an extra name, on my finger there was a ring and inside the house there was a man. Oops! Who is going to take the lead? That was my first reaction. I knew nothing about my husband, he knew nothing about me. The least you ask, the less you know, but was it the least you care? No, I was determined to make our merger successful. With steps withdrawn by each one of us, we managed to launch our journey.

I never told you what I think of love, family and marriage.

Love, is a combination of mutual respect, understanding, care and ... love!

Family is a group of people getting together in tears and joy, and asking about each other.

Marriage is a partnership built on love with the goal to make a family.

That was what we started, with the intentions to move on, and the determination to carry on, it happened. It was the perfect life! It was one that would last for years and forever, anyone wanting perfection should love these components.

I was on the right track. My sins were forgiven with my marriage, and reconciliation took place with my father.

Life was beautiful, and dues were paid off. What else would I want? Soon after my older brother who left years back when I was home, came to visit with his son. Through different occasions, between father, older sister and brother visiting, it started really feeling like a family or rather a second family. A second family not by who comes first but rather another group.

Another dream of mine was on its way, here we go, a new beginning full of different adventures and people that come together to give me a new family.

Chapter 7

When love finds us, we don't turn our back on it! That is my mission in life. Probably it's because I am a loving person, probably because I believe that love can steer the world, and probably because I enjoy seeing people falling in love, and regardless of the outcome of that love. There are no guarantees in life, and nothing lasts forever even if it is based on love. Relationships are harder than any business to maintain and it is up to both parties to keep that relationship alive. Mostly, it is a general rule, but everything in life has roots, and depending on the roots, occasional situations, and buried feeling, our attitude, character, and way of thinking differ.

At a specific time, we look around, and we see only the future. It doesn't mean that we are over the past, it rather means we have blocked the past. Usually, this happens when we reach an optimum level of pain, disappointment and deception. When pain penetrates every cell of our body, goes through our veins, starts giving unexplained medical conditions; when we start living the illusion that pain is a living particle, and at that time we can see it and touch it; when we expect sunshine, and, over and over again, one disappointment after the other; when we expect again and again someone to stand out there and pull us away, when we feel, the more we trust, the more we are deceived; we look around, we see smiles, we see fake smiles, we fake smiles back … at this point, we are on the peak point of conflicts between mind and soul. The mind functions rationally with data, dates and consequences, as for the soul longing for a two-way love, it is lost. At this peak point, a decision must be made.

We cannot remain at the peak point, we have to go either with the mind or with the soul, and either way, it is the point of no return.

To me, men are all nice, especially if we can reach the point of understanding. Physically some are different than others; emotionally, they show it in different ways and that depends on how they see romance, how they protect their ego that stands in the way of expressing their feelings, and probably how much they have to offer on a materialistic or emotional level. On a materialistic level, it starts with how much they have but it has nothing to do with generosity and their style of life. Some could have nothing to offer but enjoy the social life and seek to enlarge their network, while others will have plenty to share, yet they prefer not to; on an emotional level, treating their other half is at the heart of marriage. A flower can buy a woman's heart while at times a bouquet can mean nothing. Women, in my opinion, are born to be loved, men as well, but if a man does not know how to make his partner feel like his queen, eventually, the charm in the relationship will dwindle.

In general, women are more sensitive and emotionally driven. That is why we see tears shed in all occasions. That is why they build dreams farther than they can see. Their dreams are to see their kids graduating, getting married, their grand kids playing on the patio, eating their baked goodies, running in the house, etc. ... Men do dream, but mainly, of financial security, the house paid off, cars bought, education, insurance, etc. ... and of course, is that the last woman I will have in my life? That is where the scale plays its role, the scale that balances a couple's relationship. I am not saying men are not romantic, or they don't enjoy the moment, I am saying they tend to shift their focus to the long term security of the family.

I believe, there is plenty of love in marriage, shown and presented in each individual's own ways, but my question is, where is the sparkle that was there the time a couple met?

Once, my dad told me, those who have no marital family conflicts, will face struggle to co-adjust conflicts. Indeed that was my problem. Marriage is a big word, with a big commitment and the commitment falls on both parties. First, there should be pre-nuptial communication, on how, what, where, who, and when. Yes too many questions but not the reason behind the success of the marriage; the second point, the role of the woman in marriage; and the third point, how ready the man is for marriage.

Discussing the third point directly, what is the role of the man in the marital institution?

Is the man in charge of all financial obligations? Does the man have a role in romantic obligations? Does the man have a role in keeping the sparkle alive? Does the man have a role in children's lives? Does the man have a role in keeping up his wife's self-confidence? Etc. ...

Going back to the first point, the questions must be asked, not as an agreement, but rather to safeguard the understanding on where this marriage is heading and who is heading the ship. If there are no goals to reach, there will never be strategies to get there, and here is where the emptiness among the couple starts residing.

Being a woman raised in the Middle East, the norm is to get married and be led. The man is the head of the house, he is in charge and takes full responsibility. Some countries have developed to accept the woman as the leader, but it is considered offensive to many men and communities. Men get married to make families, women are there to raise the kids and make things succeed.

Unfortunately, I have never been that woman. I cherish the family, but I want to lead or take part in the leadership. Once a man told me, the man is the head of the woman, my answer was, men are by the side of the woman and if they deserve it, she will allow them in her heart! He was offended, I don't blame him; that is the mentality in our community. Some might agree, others might disagree, but it will take generations for people to change. It is acceptable for men to flirt, have female friends but not acceptable for women to do so. I am heading to one question, do men change after marriage, and do women change after marriage?

Men, when they marry, they feel it's an achievement. Therefore, many feel they have accomplished their role, especially if they have secured all materialistic and marital standards obligations, they believe it's their right to live their life. While women, once married, many let go of beautifying themselves, they incline to care for the children, house, birthdays etc. and they tend to forget that their man is on the loose. Suddenly, problems start arising, but wait, it did not happen suddenly. As it takes years to build a relationship, it takes less years to tear it apart; and those who experienced insecurity in their lives, this becomes a wake-up call for them, and puts them on an alert.

This point leads to my situation ... what started in a bed of roses, crumbled on a field of grass. Why roses? The relationship started in seconds, flourished in minutes and bloomed overnight. Why grass? Because grass spreads on a wider surface and lasts longer than flowers ... this is marriage, like roses it blooms quickly, then it's up to the grass to see how far and long it can spread and last.

I do not believe my husband and I got to know each other the right way. I do believe though, that we both went with the flow of coming from the same background, being in the same business, and that both being in a home away from home played a positive role in bringing us together. Were we in love? We sure did, and I can speak for myself, I surely was. Was there a quick decision in marriage? Was there a get to know each other phase that decided the future of the couple? Were the elements available that must be present in order for the relationship to succeed? Many will answer yes.

I investigated the issue of after-marriage concerns with many men and women. What were your pre-nuptial concerns? Men's overall answers were based on finances, obligations and only few answered about romance and kids, one of them was concerned about his wife gaining weight or having her as the last woman in his life. As for the women, mostly, the answers were about successful marriage, romance, long-term love, family, children, grandchildren, education, what to do, etc. ... many on the other hand were concerned about after-marriage intimate relations, weight gain, how to balance between home and kids, and I am not discussing working women yet. I do believe that men are romantic, I do believe that they hide their feelings, those I do not worry about, my concern is with those who are not romantic and do not work on themselves, for them and then for their partner; this last part, working on ourselves apply for both of us women and men, when we look at each other's character and notice that one of us has to be the mature one.

When either a man or a woman takes on that oath saying, I do, they should be ready for the "I do" subsequent. I believe that the matrimonial phase starts after the wedding, honeymoon, and even few months after. It is on that morning when they wake up and see each other's habits as is, away from the outside world, they look at each other and say, wow that is the person I am spending the rest of my life with! He is the last person I will flirt with, the last person I will share my stories, ideas and bed with, the last person I will be passionate about!

Now you know, it was love and not passion. For love to survive, my dear friends, there is a recipe, called passion. Many of us after the marriage, forget the little tiny detail called, "What I liked about you." I slept near my spouse and woke up near a monster. They argue, they have an opinion, they are not interested now in the intimate moment, they make each other feel like everyone else in the room when in public, they had a long day at work, they are facing a difficult phase, they have been driving, cooking, cleaning all day, they have been ... this was about the typical working man, and housewife and mother.

That is the first phase of the marital conflict, when the hug becomes rational and not emotional. Sadly, we can all fall in the trap of marriage as a partnership and lose its essence, especially when the days become a routine, and no longer innovative crispy moments taking place here and there. Well, one should never forget the reason that united the couple, and definitely never forget that the reason was the beginning of tomorrow. When someone decides to marry, the life they lived yesterday no longer exists. That is why they call it a new chapter if not a new book. It is a new day, new and more people joining our network, new concepts, a decision made by two instead of one, negotiation and communication techniques, etc. ... and mainly new challenges that consist of keeping the spirit of love floating between each other and spreading under that roof that is uniting them.

First and foremost, when a couple unites, it is to make a family. Under normal conditions, and if there are no major issues in our past that might stand in the way of the future and hinder it, we carry the past and our friends from the past along, respectfully to our future. As long as, again, respectfully, we move on with the understanding that we want to build a new beginning, and a new life. The question resides when one of the couple rejects the past of the other half and its connections, and for no valid reason ... that is the ignition of concern on a social level.

Then, the question is always, and it goes to both men and women, where is the man/woman I married?

Chapter 8

The first couple years of marriage were heavy, between mixed feelings, adjusting to each other's character and getting to know each other, days were not as expected. I believe the fact that I was not working, did not make things easier for me. It was a while since I was financially dependent. I got pregnant with my first daughter, got busy with the pregnancy, my dad came to visit, my brother joined with his younger son, and we had a great time. That is where my dad opened up to me and told me that now he was at peace, considering I got married. A day before the due date in 1992, the big earthquake hit Los Angeles. I was terrified and anxious for her safety. Right after we got clearance to go on the freeway, we drove to the hospital, and that is where the doctor recommended I stay in and prepared me for the big moment, the delivery. Throughout my pregnancy, all I was thinking about was my mother, during her pregnancy with me, and now at the final moments, I was thinking about the last moments on the delivery table, before she was having me, and wishing her presence with me. I prayed for her, for her forgiveness and prayed to see my daughter in my arms. The next morning, in the early hours, I had my first baby girl. I called her Vanessa, Greek translation of butterfly, she was the soul coming out of the cocoon to bring good luck to the house. She filled my life with joy and will to survive; she filled the house with happiness and things were centered on her. She was the perfect child, with big eyes and black silky hair. I would never have enough of looking at her, carrying her, playing with her and like any first child, she developed quickly but showed very bright signs comparing her to children her age. My dad came to visit, she was around forty days with activities of a three month old baby. Right after, my family came to visit from Lebanon and things were better among us as well. She had the spirit of an angel, sent to add blessings to the house, indeed she did. Nothing mattered to me anymore, not with her presence. By eight months, she was talking three languages, and she made her first step, the day of her first birthday. By age fourteen months, we had to travel back home to Lebanon to finalize our green card papers. It was a great trip except it was crowned with news that broke my heart, my dad had an advanced stage of brain cancer, and his days left with us were numbered. Luckily, I was able to film the last supper with him among us. Unluckily, he was not able to attend Vanessa's christening. After that, he was hospitalized, and shortly after, he went into a coma. It was sad seeing the end of an energetic man who was full of life … I guess, this is life. There is a time for everything to end. After checking with his doctor, he informed us of no time limit for his coma, I had seen enough and it was too painful, so we decided to go back to the States. The second day after we got there, we received a call, that it was over; my dad was resting in heaven. His pain was eased, but mine missing him never did. Dad, I am sorry, I was not there to hug you goodbye, but I guess I still feel your last hug, at home before the hospital, and I had a last supper movie that reminded me of you at the dinner table, as I always remembered. In my heart I carry your love, on my shoulder your hand and on my nightstand your picture. Rest in peace, alongside my mom, the woman I never met, give her my warm thoughts and love … hope you were both proud of me!

Life has no rules, our age has no time frame, and it is not about the days we lived, rather it's about the life we lived. I was sad for all my losses, but God blessed me with an angel, for her, and for her only, I will take care of the future, and all I can be in charge of. Shortly after, I got pregnant, I thought it was meant for me to get over my sadness, to replace the loss of my father with the birth of another baby. Instead I discovered I had a Hydatidiform mole or a molar pregnancy. In short, cancer of the placenta, that if well treated and detected on time, it goes with the treatment and the suction curettage (D and C) performed. After around four months of testing and close follow up by the doctors, the D and C was performed. With a strict note from the doctor not to get pregnant, close medical follow up to ensure the cancer was benign and did not spread beyond the placenta to the kidney, liver and spine, after a few months of testing, the doctors confirmed that I was clear of all damaged cells, and I was given a chance to have another baby. This phase was emotionally damaging to me, especially after losing my dad under the cancer umbrella. So I got pregnant again, six months after the D and C. Being emotionally tired, I was supposed to take a longer break, but since my anxiety was related to pregnancy, I preferred to ensure my daughter Vanessa had a sibling. So here goes a nine month phase starting off on the left foot. I was determined to have that baby, with all the love I could have and faith towards this pregnancy; I decided to set all concerns aside and be happy. I started the prenatal care, with it a new problem with the insurance documents. This was the last problem I needed and going through different financial means caused a lot of pressure on me. Yet, I told myself, what is important is the baby's health. I moved on, more determined to go through with the pregnancy, but no matter how determined I was, I couldn't delete from my mind the molar pregnancy, and it pre-occupied my thoughts. All I wanted was to hear the baby's heartbeat and see him/her on the monitor. Finally, that phase passed, and that day came like a blessing. As if it was today, I remember my tears falling from happiness, I remember myself looking at the screen while the doctor was measuring the fetus and thanking God for this gift.

I went home that day carrying in my womb a gift from God, nothing could stand in the way of my happiness. I was ecstatic. With full energy, I faced the rest of the pregnancy. But I guess all the stress I lived prior to and in the beginning of the pregnancy had to be paid off. I started feeling weird, so while visiting the doctor four months in, we discovered I had diabetes. More tests on the go, and they put me on insulin with a strict diet in order to protect me and my baby. Another earthquake hit Los Angeles, between my pregnancy, the earthquake, and the insurance problems my world was shaken. Is there enough a woman can take?

I started the insulin treatment, along with a strict diet, and said to myself, I will go through with this pregnancy. But I guess I was tired, and things started creating tension in the house. After a short-tempered incident in the house in front of Vanessa, she started stuttering. Vanessa was very attached to her dad, as he was as well, he used to help take care of her, dance with her, play with her, prepare her milk shakes, etc. ... so as she added joy to my heart, she did give her dad a motivational push. I guess the short-tempered incident shook her out of fear and disappointment from her idol. By then, she was about two years old and she was fluently speaking three languages. I guess being more mature than her age, made her feel the pressure in the house and affected her speech. I was referred to a psychologist who taught me how to pretend play with her and reassure her that all will be fine. That was a short phase, before my bigger health set back, where I started showing signs of pre-eclampsia. At that time, I was supposed to be monitored daily. So I started going daily to the hospital, with Vanessa, her toys and meals, spending four hours on the monitor, and ensuring Mommy and baby are ok.

By then, I was numb, I did not know what to think or pray for. All I asked for was a baby sister for Vanessa, regardless of the outcome of the pregnancy. With full monitoring, careful care for Vanessa, insulin shots, and a strict diet, I couldn't but wonder why is this happening?

Was this phase the "to be continued" of a previous one? Am I to join my mother, or have a still baby? Wasn't the sequence of misfortunate events due to break? I couldn't and wouldn't ask more questions, I just carried with me the thoughts till judgment day. I couldn't not think about the future, what if, what if and what if ... instead I tried to remain fixated on one point. Why would God take away from me his gift ... the gift of God? Something inside me was pushing me to remain strong and believe in a higher power. Something was pushing me to have hope, faith and plan the future. So I tried pushing away all negativity, and made plans for a family vacation to give us, as a family, a second chance. We did, my husband, myself and Vanessa took a vacation together. We discussed our issues and concerns, we discussed the reasons behind the conflicts and mainly that is where my husband prepared for the move to Lebanon. By then, I had already requested to move to another State. The recession was at a peak time and the two earthquakes we witnessed during and between pregnancies truly made me uncomfortable. So my husband requested to come during my pregnancy to Lebanon, to check the economic situation, and, if he felt that it was worth the move, a joint decision would be taken. As agreed, after we went back home from the vacation, he went to Lebanon and came back with a positive view. The only pre-nuptial agreement or discussion we ever had, was me never wanting to go back to Lebanon. But when my husband came back, he was sure and assertive that we, as a family, would be better off in Lebanon, and me wanting to have a family, and wanting my kids to live among aunties, uncles and grandparents, having the earthquakes shaking and the recession still ongoing, I gave the move some thought under one condition. The condition was that we would give the family a one year grace period. We move to Lebanon but if we were not happy, he promised the move back to the States. We agreed to move six months after delivery.

I still had months to go, but meanwhile I started getting excited with the move idea although it was not on my agenda. I guess there are times in life, when we start thinking differently, and those times start when the "I" becomes a "we." Despite all the incidents that took place in the past, in Lebanon, all I could think of was to share my beautiful Vanessa and hopefully her sibling with my friends, his friends, and both our families. I started dreaming of us being there, changing our lifestyle, living the way I lived under my dad's roof, with a full house. I wanted my kids to grow where I grew and take the best of both worlds, of both families and friends. I wanted everyone to have changed, the ghosts to be gone, and love be spread. I wanted my kids to visit both grandparents and be spoiled by them. I wanted the husband I married back, the person I decided to build a life and future with. I wanted a lot, but nothing more than love.

As agreed, we decided the move, but first we had to go through the pregnancy for our dreams to be complete. I was in my last weeks, the preparation started for my delivery, home and Vanessa preparation. No matter how far I could go with my dreams, the preparations were limited.

Time was clicking, close to 40 weeks, my due date, I was done, tired from insulin injections, exhausted from all concerns, and I just wanted one thing, to hold my baby in my arms and put this phase behind me. I prepared Vanessa's things in order at home, I showered her, and all three of us went to the hospital with my best friends.

I settled Vanessa in her play pan to sleep through the night. I went to the next room where they prepared me. The doctor estimated the delivery time for six hours, so he induced labor at one o'clock after midnight. I wanted everything to be done by the time Vanessa woke up. As planned, by six-thirty in the morning, like a sunshine glowing on me, I was holding my baby girl in my arms, a true gift from God, Tiffany, and that is the meaning of her name.

Chapter 9

The next months after Tiffany's birth were exciting and tough. With the decision to move back to Lebanon by the time Tiffany would be six months, and Tiffany having infant sleep Apnea at birth, I didn't know how I would have gone through the days without the help of Vanessa, and saying she was only two years and seven months. I knew infant sleep Apnea, Tiffany's case, would disappear in a few months, still, the idea just kept me alert. I used to speak to Vanessa at my level almost, asking her to watch her sister, read to her, etc. … while I shower or nap, and giving her instructions on steps to follow in case Tiffany forgot to breathe!

Did I overload this child with responsibilities heavier than she could handle? I don't think so, I believe our children give us signs when they are overwhelmed or tired, as for Vanessa, she was so excited with the baby's arrival since pregnancy. I remember when I used to take her to the mall, she used to put baby clothes on my belly in order to decide whether they fit or not, and whether the baby would like them or not.

Like many other mothers out there with a toddler and an infant, my life was busy non-stop and all my focus was centered on both daughters; and with Tiffany's birth, I felt my life was complete. I was the happiest ever, and I think since then, I never stopped being happy. Looking at both my daughters reminded me of how blessed I was. It gave me this energy and power that made me feel on top of the world. I used to fear to close my eyes and miss the sight of them. I guess, having them replaced all the memories of the past, I had no time to think about anyone or anything else, in addition to not wanting to jinx the present with undesirable memories. I became a mom during the day and an owl at night watching over them. My life was alive finally, and I did not dare wish for anything else, fearing the trade for what I had. Peaking at my life a few years back, from family, to friends, to lifestyle, it was all swapped to gaining my sister, brother and family back, in addition to my daughters whom I believe were my good luck charms.

Around that time, another farewell was due, the move to Lebanon. I was not concerned about the adjustment phase as much as I was worried about the phase itself. Additionally, when it comes to my sister, I finally had gotten to know her, see her, and with both of us having children around the same age, I felt it was an addition for us to get closer. My sister and I did not share much in common, we drifted apart with her move as I was around nine years old, and we were both adults when we met again. So, getting her close again and finding common points was my goal. She was dedicated to the church since she was a teenager and with time, and her marrying an Orthodox priest, she got more involved which was a major point to me, since I was truly far from that field. Anyways, the truth is, I was used to goodbyes, but I promised her to visit and remain in touch, and I promised her that our kids will have a better relationship, and that I would ensure they would be in touch. Before I moved, she started having problems with her husband and my aunt helped her with the kids. As for my brother and his wife, we promised each other to remain in touch.

I was not ready to leave them, but I guess I had no choice.

Farewell, LA, the land of my dreams, thank you for hosting me, but I'm moving on, back to where everything started. More farewells to friends and family, and with all the mixed feelings I had in my heart and soul, I had to trust destiny one more time.

All packed and ready to go, we took the plane back home to the country I promised I would never step in again … it was weird, I wanted to ask my husband what is it that he had done to convince me, but I guess fate played its role. My heart was crushed for my sister, brother and their families, thinking about the next time I would see them again, but on the other hand I wanted to go back home, to Lebanon, I wanted my daughters to be among family members, I wanted them to see where I grew up and get to know my friends. I wanted to share with the whole world my daughters, my happiness and pride. I wanted a fresh start with my community, away from ghosts, disregarding gossip, and only a peaceful life.

From one house to another, waiting for our shipment of furniture to reach Lebanon, and finally, we got settled.

It was a very busy and hectic time, on top of having a three-year-old, a six-month-old, moving, and finding a school for Vanessa, our social life had started. We had to be ready for it, and we had to be involved. Both my husband and I had a load on our shoulders. He had to take care of the business and I had to manage the internal affairs. Indeed, that is what it started to feel like, a corporation! The story of every marriage.

When people, including myself, speak about life abroad, and compare it to life in Lebanon, one thing is always mentioned, the beauty of the country, help services offered in-house and outside, and the mess we got used to! Like every country, it has both sides of life, and despite all issues in the country, I enjoyed living there. The first stage was a bit cumbersome. I had no help in the house, it was a big house in size, with a garden, and it was on the ground floor. View the fact that I had no help in the house, and the overprotective nature I developed with the birth of both my daughters, the comfort of my daughters became a priority, and especially when Vanessa was enrolled at school and she had to be there on time. This was the first hurdle abused in terms of the unity of our family. While I was waiting on the house and daughters, cooking, changing diapers, baking goodies and bread, cleaning, organizing events, reading, singing, dancing, driving to activities, etc. ... my husband had to take part in the social community during the week. The weekends, we did socialize as a family, but mainly his side of friends and colleagues. In the beginning I told myself, he needed to do so, thinking he was away for a long while, socializing will help him on a personal and social level. Was I fine with it? Well, I did not complain about it. Firstly, I was fully engaged in my daughters' lives that nothing else mattered and secondly, it was not a choice. That was a minus one point on my behalf, but he did not object, and that was a minus two for him on my calculations, simply because, regardless of the fact that Lebanon has been my home since ever, I was feeling freshly off the boat, considering the past. My husband, as you remember, never asked me about my past. He knew one thing, the condition of no return to Lebanon, and where are we now? In Lebanon. So, I granted him the first layaway mistake. At times, it hurt a lot, I wept through the nights, but my ego would not allow me to argue. What hurt more than his social habits, was the lack of contact during the days. This was not a recent habit, it had been the same in the States, but view the style of life, my ego, and the move, now I started feeling the emptiness, and especially probably, because of the social life he had during the week days. As you remember, the reason behind our move, was above all, the conflict we had during my pregnancy with Tiffany. So this distance between us has been taking place for quite some time. The husband I had in the States, or rather the father that was present in his daughters' lives, did not move with us to Lebanon. He became the typical Middle Eastern father, with limited duties, in addition to not being able to connect socially with my friends and family. This made things more difficult, and the distance between us grew more. I was never an argumentative person, and this is the minus two for me. I was raised in a house with my step-mother with the understanding that women do not argue, but what I forgot to remember, that characteristics are situational. I view the results there, and in both cases, her and my father, never argued about the ghosts, they avoided the subject. Was it the right thing? Not only that, in the Middle East overall, an argumentative woman is a threat to the family. Couple times I tried discussing calmly the situation, and the discussion did not end positively. That was another reason for me to avoid stirring "dirt."

Having children is an expansion to life as a whole, but life does not end there. Children are not the responsibility of the woman only, children are there to be shared between both parents. The load was fully on me, not that I would have let go for any reason, but I would have enjoyed a co-partnership. As you notice, things were calm, but not to be rocked! Shortly after, the permanent live-in help arrived; and days after days, the routine settled in. My husband started travelling to Europe for business, it was normal; what was odd, was that one time after the other, I stopped crying every time he flew away. The corporation was still standing, but was it prospering? Although I was happily busy with my daughters, I started feeling the distance more and more, and wished we never moved back to this country. I never felt a local, never was a housewife, never believed in love only, never enjoyed a classic life, and was not like any other woman. I do, on the other hand, cherish my daughters and embrace marriage because of them. But clearly, this was the wrong reason. The journey I dreamt about with my move back to Lebanon was not as expected, and I started creating a comfort zone for me and my daughters. With time, life was more limited to the daily events while trying to accommodate ourselves within what we had. My family connections, despite the pretend reconciliation, still carried the debris of the past, which came back to me even with every little incident. My husband, not being the perfect sociable person, did not help. My friends, they were here and available, but my husband preferred a limited social life, which limited the encounters. As for my brother and sister abroad, I tried remaining in touch as much as possible. My brother kept on moving from one place to the other, as for my sister, her life with her husband started falling apart badly, and with time, she took her children and moved to the monastery of the church she belonged to. I tried to keep in touch around that time, but with her being in a monastery, it was not easy to do so, especially when problems happened quickly, while I was not in daily contact with her. Not being there for her, again and again, made me feel very bad. I did not want to go back in time and analyze what had happened, but again, I failed her, and this time for personal reasons. My personal situation could not afford an additional hassle and she was receiving the best support from my aunt. Deep inside, till today, I feel I failed her. Was I worried that I could not take charge of a very big responsibility or was it that I did not have enough support to take on that responsibility? Irrelevant of the reason, I failed my sister again.

Anyways, I tried moving on, amongst the many paths of joy with my own children, guilt about my sister, and concerns about my own social and family connections, I had to be strong, for me and others, letting the days judge me.

One day, around nine o'clock in the morning, my phone rang. I was doing the housework. It was my husband, not a habit of his. I was concerned, I answered. He was checking on me! That was weird. Again, he called fifteen minutes after, this time I told him I was worried, he insisted that he was checking on me. Another fifteen minutes, he called again, I insisted on knowing the reason behind the call.

His partner took the phone, asked me to sit down, I knew something was badly wrong. He announced to me the death of my sister. Time froze. "Which one?" I said, not that it made a difference, I love them both equally, and the answer was, the sister you have in the States.

Bye bye, the sister I never had, the one I failed. I refused to go to the funeral, she was gone. Time stopped for me, life consisted of ongoing breathing and no goal. I could not express myself, I could not wear black, and I could not mourn her. I was the one who needed to be mourned on, I was lost, dead, angry, and with many questions ...

Where are you, GOD? Why did you take my mother at twenty-six? Why did you take my sister at thirty-six? Where are you? I need answers!

Chapter 10

The loss of my sister was a slap on the face. Life froze the moment I heard the news, with all its interests. Nothing mattered anymore, other than the inside of my house. I put all my focus on what I had, instead of what I lost. I could not show anger, sadness, or any kind of emotion; instead I rearranged my life systematically. My heart had only maternal love, as for my mind, it started functioning rationally. Life became a calculation of reality and a miscalculation of expectations. I could not afford any more surprises, I let go of the outside world!

The loss of my sister brought the memories to the surface, and for the first time, I faced myself with the facts and realities. I started putting in front of me, every incident that happened to me since birth, one at a time, analyzing it, and starting with one statement, things happen for a reason. I was never able to reach the reason behind every event, instead I convinced myself to reach a very important conclusion: I am not to blame, and it just happened that I was in the wrong place at the right time to know, hear, see and feel.

I decided to be the master of my own destiny and take charge of my life. I started with my daughters. I protected them from human pain like a mother gorilla. I raised men in women figures. I convinced them that their destiny is in their hands, I told them to live their life openly and not to be ashamed of any actions they may decide to take or make; I told them they will not marry till they have a degree, till they became financially independent and succeed; I told them to guide their life with passion and not love; and I told them that they can reach any goal they put their mind into and mainly that I was there for them regardless of what mistakes they make, because mistakes are just the stepping stones to success; and I told them to spread their wings wide open and fly as high as they can reach.

As for my husband, I tried working on our relationship. I created moments trying to change him, it was not easy. He was sinking into being a Middle Eastern man, and I was determined to pull him back to the surface. Mistake, changing our partner is going against the flow. So I tried going with the flow and that is where I sank. I was not the housewife many men would dream about, in terms of limiting myself to raising a family, house chores, family chores and staying at home. Not that there is anything wrong with being a housewife, I have great respect for those on a twenty-four hour service, but I always believed that those who can manage to care for their family, and would like to work, they should be granted that right. When it comes to me, especially, that when me and my husband met, I was living alone in my own apartment abroad, and I was in charge of myself, which means, it was not strange to him, me not fitting in the perfect housewife zone. I did not mind his lack of interest in family, travelling, gatherings, outings, movie nights, lack of romance, etc. ... but with time, our socializing circle started shrinking; I felt the need to break through. Change of habits and pattern in life are not easy, people can adjust but they may not adapt. View the nature of my past, working in different fields all at once when I was in the States, and being successful on my own, I started feeling useless. I was working since I was seventeen, and I always felt there was a whole world out there waiting for me. I always wanted a huge family but I never saw myself jobless. With the routine of the house, in addition to the move, in addition to the loss of my sister and, to the new resolution I set to myself, I felt the need for change. I couldn't find the passion in our relationship. I felt I needed to get to know the man I married all over again. At times, I wondered whether I was dreaming about a passionate relationship or whether it existed, all I knew, I was passionately driven. Nothing I did, I accomplished with a simple love. I always added a little passion to flavor any tasks, from baking, to household, to dealing with people and to the outside world. That was part of my resolution, to keep passion alive, and the determination to continue. I reshuffled my emotions, and with a new energy, I started with my husband. I told myself happiness starts within the house and filters outwards, I had to try again.

Then, I ran a little flashback and statistics on the history in my family, if my birth-mom passed at twenty-six and having four kids, my sister passed at thirty-six with three kids, statistics said, my turn would come at forty-six since I had two kids. I had to benefit from the time with my husband and two daughters since I was only thirty. I would not spend the time calculating, instead, I would make the best out of it.

I started involving myself in social activities, I got in touch with my old friends, colleagues in motherhood, and with my husband's friends. As for my husband, he preferred not to take part. The new me, did not force the issue, instead I formed two different social lives. The inner revolution created in me a passion towards life. I was always a passionate person, but I believe the excessive loss factor, and being in charge of my daughters now, made my passion towards life even stronger. I guess when people lose loved ones, they keep on sinking till they reach the bottom; after that, it's a critical phase, I call it sedation, as if the feelings are numb. It's a decisive phase, it's about feeling guilty towards the loved ones we lost, and lack of interest in life. It is similar to someone sinking in the ocean, they see the bottom reflecting death in which the pain ends; death at that phase is the salvation itself, where we live a painless life. If we reach the sedation phase, and seeing the refuge there, it will be very difficult for us to see the light on top. The darkness of the bottom, despite how scary it could be, will protect us from human pain and attract us to stay. Loneliness will become our friendly environment. At that time, we need true passion to pull us up to the surface. And in my case, it was the voices of my daughters. Every time I heard their voices, I longed to survive more, and indeed, they were the ones who pulled me up. I call that phase a struggle phase, when our feelings struggle between the two ends. I did succeed to see the light, although I choked on many feelings on my way up, but I wanted to seek the surface and finally I reached it. I call this phase salvation. If we do not cross the path of mourning, we can never reach serenity. I found out that serenity does not mean forgetfulness, it rather means acceptance of a specific situation and loss. My salvation phase involved the determination to keep the family together, and branched on developing myself in different activities. I realized by then that my husband and I had different views of what a family is. To him, it was the inside of the home. To me, it was developing the inside of home while maintaining and growing a social life. Both probably are good, but as said earlier, one cannot change their partner, especially if they are not interested. Life between two people, husband and wife, is a compromise. After facing the adaptation phase, which is a major dilemma, both must give and take in order to grow on the same wave. Unfortunately, by me creating two lives, one with him and another with my daughters, I created rifts in the family. I had no choice; my passion towards life had always been part of my character. One more time, I stood alone, and one step after the other, I found myself in charge of a daycare that was opening across the floor from my house. I could have gone back to the jewelry business, either with the family or with my husband, but my attachment to both my daughters was growing more and more every day. Instead I chose to volunteer across the floor, in the daycare where I had enrolled my daughter Tiffany, and slowly after, I took charge of it after proving myself in a field I knew nothing about, other than raising my two beautiful daughters by the book. The owner of the daycare was a sharp self-made businessman with a vision. The daycare, in 1997, was the first of his developments, along with a school. He believed in others' potential and delegated unlimited tasks for development. I proved myself, and together we walked the journey.

 My self-development, although at a daycare level, although with my daughter, and although on the same floor of my house, made my husband uncomfortable, and created conflicts between us. I enjoyed what I was doing so much, and I couldn't let go. More ups and downs were faced, but I was determined to go on. I was a business woman, before I was a wife and a mother, and I found myself there. So, no way back was my plan. Instead, within the same year, I started helping at school, as well as a volunteer. More tasks were assigned to me, and more dedicated and involved I became to the business side in the world of education. I never lacked any duty towards my daughters, husband, or home, instead I generated more energy to fulfill more. In addition to more tasks, I faced more rifts in the house. Our conflicts grew, which set us more apart. I knew we weren't heading in the right direction, because of specific terms my husband used during our quarrels; so I visited our church priest who confirmed to me that, in our religion and country, the law stood by the father in terms of custody of children below the age of fourteen. At fourteen, children would be called to court for interrogation, in order to decide on their custody. I could never imagine my life away from my daughters, so, I continued working, but with a low profile. I had no intentions to raise my daughters away from their father, and I never wanted them to live in a broken home, or feel the tension of parental conflicts. I kept the environment smooth, as much as possible. Days went by, I thought with time, my husband would accept my choice, instead things got worst. I was convinced though that work was not the main reason behind the conflicts, therefore, to me the job became my security. More schools to build, with more tasks I chose to take on, the girls were growing, and I was succeeding more and more. I enrolled both daughters in our school, and we rented a house nearby. By then, we had closed the first daycare. A relative of mine stood by me financially, and I opened a daycare in partnership with the owner of the school and previous daycare. It was my first baby business. It was very successful, but I was stretched very thin between the daycare, schools and family. Around this time, the owner's brother moved to Lebanon with his family, he moved to head the school where my daughters were enrolled. We got introduced, we started working together, and he offered me a full time position. It was a tempting and tough decision, knowing I could be with my daughters and around them all the time but I had never worked in an institution with many people. I was always my own master and I was always my own team. Additionally, I had to make a decision about the daycare, to close it or to entrust it to someone, and to me, it was a very delicate issue, kids at a very early age must be in very safe hands. It was a dilemma, a big dilemma, but I was given a week to decide. So I used the scale system, on one side I added the positives and on the other side I added the negatives. My relationship with my husband was put on the line, therefore I thought that being in a school with my children and living by their schedule would help ease the pressure; I was concerned about getting bored in a limited environment but on the other hand, I got to be with my daughters at all times; I was never a team player, I used to believe many will delay a process that could be achieved by one, but I thought it might be challenging enough for me … and last, should I leave a whole world of business to be stuck in one business? My questions brought to mind different answers and thoughts … it was a foggy week, and I had to think about what I wanted as well. My husband never thought that a volunteer job across the floor will get me here; the insecurity between us made me want to create a "ME" elsewhere; I have always been in the world of business; I was not a woman who can just stand behind a man, he can stand by me if he wants; working provided an open social life for me; financial security, and mainly, I will not draw back to satisfy anyone!

My family does come first … but I started thinking, if I love someone, I wish them happiness, but I do not wish them doing what makes me happy. I believe that was the problem I was living with at home with my husband. A family consists of many members, there is a family priority that comes first, but then, an individual priority that is a main factor in the happiness and continuity of the whole, after all, a whole becomes a hole without the special ones that created it, and sadly, the rift and hole inside the house kept on growing!

Chapter 11

I took the position in opposition with my husband and that was the beginning of a new chapter. He was not happy about my decision, nor did I feel I was making him happy overall. I started questioning myself, where were we heading? How were we heading there? Why were we together? Did he love me? Did he hate me? Did he want me? Did he miss me? What made a couple? And I wasn't questioning myself yet. Life between us was suffocated, as if it was under a spell, why wasn't he fighting for me? Why was he not attracted to me?

Relationships cannot grow silently, they require hours of talk, disagreement, discussions, fights, reconciliations, understandings, acceptance, letting go, etc. ... but as well relationships require above all, a want-to-be together, and that feeling was dormant. I never knew what went wrong and when did things go wrong, and mainly did we want-to-be together or were we just together?

Nights and days of silence, nonchalance, and routine. A relation living in the darkness and nurtured by indifference. How far can we go? And why are we ignoring each other?

Where was the flame that brought us together? Why were there no more roses? Where did the romance go? Why weren't there new memories? Where were the cute touches, kisses, hugs? Where were the passionate moments?

More and more questions went through my mind, but more importantly was what was going through my heart ...

My days started with my daughters and ended with them. Whether my husband was in town or abroad, I used to come home from work with my daughters during the week, finish the house chores, homework, dinner, shower and all their needs for that day and the next day, then to bed ... all three of us.

Those were the good days, I involved myself at work, it was fun, and productive. My days were filled with different tasks, as for the nights, they were pure silence. All I could hear was my daughters' breathing, and my heart beating. And slowly, my heartbeat was weakening, and vanishing in the valleys; I used to hear it melt through the wind and the leaves of the trees; I even saw it finding its way under the soil. Why was my heart going there? What was happening? It turned out, while I was taking care of my daughters, and involving myself at work, I forgot my soul. I looked in the mirror, and that was not me. It was a picture of me, but heavier. Where was my smile? What happened to the sparkle in my eyes? What happened to the glow on my face? Well, it turned out that, I as well, let go of myself. I got busy taking care of everything but myself. I forgot the happy-go-lucky girl somewhere along the road, and ignored nurturing her soul. I forgot that one cannot live without love, passion, and stolen flirts here and there; I forgot that if one does not love self, they cannot offer love; and I forgot that one should be cherished, and cuddled, and loved etc. ... to be able to love back. The passion inside me steered towards my daughters and tasks, and forgot the most important task, myself. So I decided, if love can't be, love shall be; I owe it to myself, to rejuvenate my soul; I told myself, what I cannot live during the day, I shall live during the night. A new journey away from all stress, a mask, a beautiful lady, a dream, a true passion, and almost a reality. It was about a man every woman would dream about; he was tall, dark skin, blue eyes. It was at the beginning of the fall season, it just happened that we were both walking on the beach at sunset time, the wind picked up, and the waves got stronger. It was getting cold, I sat there on the rocks throwing the load of the day in the ocean, and suddenly, I felt someone covering my shoulders with a jacket; for a moment, and instead of looking up and checking who it was, I closed my eyes, and enjoyed the moment; then, with his soft and loving hands, he rubbed my neck and shoulders to keep me warm; again, I did not look up, I only wanted the moment to never stop; instead I looked at his hands, and I saw tenderness, age, wisdom ... I felt his passion through the shivering of his hands; I said to myself, this was the day things will turn around; for a stranger to dare to do what he has done, I was sure our souls had met somewhere, and he was here to continue the journey. I stared at his hands, I couldn't stop, he sat near me, he looked me in the eyes, he held my hand, and never let go of it ever again. It wasn't the first time we had met, but it was the first time we had seen each other. I looked him in the eyes, I couldn't blink, I lived years in moments, I saw trust, friendship, love, passion, and as well I saw emptiness, loneliness, longing for love; I rested my head on his shoulders, and there I felt the support I was missing. We stayed there for a while, gazing at the ocean, not a single word was said, and no names, phone numbers, or any contacts were exchanged. Instead, when it was time to leave, with a simple sign by the eyes, we left, saying, "See you tomorrow, at the same time." We left, looking at the rear view mirror, we were peeking at each other, the space was only physical, we both had this feeling we desired for quite some time. I was positive we were going to meet again, and I had full faith in tomorrow. I went home with my heart filled with joy, and couldn't wait till the next day. I had forgotten the feeling of being alive, I couldn't believe how quick I let go of myself, but what was important, I wasn't alone, and feelings were mutual. The next day came, impatiently I ran to meet him, he was there, sitting on our rock, but he wasn't looking at the ocean, instead he was looking at the road, where I was walking. I missed having someone waiting for me, I missed having someone looking at me this way, and missing me. I got there, I stood in front of him, and he whispered in my ears, I barely heard what he said, but feeling his lips touching my ears made my heart melt for him. We sat on our rock, he wrapped his arm around me, we held hands, and decided to meet weekly. We stayed for a couple hours, and till then we knew nothing about each other. Before we left, we took a walk by the beach, where we both admitted to each other we were married, and we both decided on one thing, we were in this situation for self and not to hurt our partners. We exchanged the first name only, no other information, and with a big hug, we left. As a woman, if a man looked at me as I walked away after being with him, it meant he cared.

And as I was walking away, I felt his looks piercing through me, reaching deep into my soul, whispering beautiful words to me. Can't wait to see you next week, he said, and keep my hand with you. His words gave me enough love to dream about till we met the next time. I couldn't wait, I couldn't stop thinking about him, whether he was missing me, thinking about me, or even coming next week. The days passed so slow, it was similar to torture, and going through the countdown, made me want to sleep till we met again.

It was the meeting day, early in the morning; I was so lost, missing him so much, I couldn't wait. I couldn't leave until I settled all and everyone. It was time, it was windy and cold, I got there, I rushed to our rock, and no one was there. I got closer, I saw something on our rock, and I saw a purple tulip with a note. I smiled, I took the note, it said, "I miss you, I will always be here waiting for you." My tears started shedding, but with great happiness, I turned around to see him standing there, I ran, I threw myself in his arms, as if I had known him for ages. Did you ever meet someone and felt you had known each other for ages? Well, that was us. It turned out he was thinking about me the same way I was thinking about him, missing me, wanting me, and couldn't wait for our meeting day. Between passion and reality, I just wanted to be in his arms till dawn, I wanted us to share something together, and to create our own memories. Although the rocks were our special place, I just wanted our moments to feel more real, so I suggested a shack in the mountain. We started looking, we found a place away from the city, close enough to remain near civilization, but far enough to ensure our privacy. The next time, we met there, a shack on the hill, with grass all around, a fireplace and cushions all around. Where is this passion taking us? I said. He answered, till we have enough of each other, and let me tell you, I miss you more every day, and I even miss you when I'm with you. Words in a soft voice, truthfulness, love, passion, I couldn't but believe him and trust him. I met many people in my life, many showed different characteristics, but no one showed them all. This man reminded me that

I was a woman, he reminded me of my beauty and charisma, he reminded me of how capable I was, and he made me feel like his queen. What was I to him? His everything, and why? Because he had everything and nothing. A big house, a wife, kids, cars, helpers, etc. ... but no one was there to ask him about his day, what he ate, who he met etc. ...

How to love a man is a very basic question, the answer is, love him from the heart. And when it comes to women, any love will do, just love her, love her, and keep on loving her. That is what I found with this man, and I offered much more. Not because he deserved more than others, first and foremost, that is how I love, I cherish my partner, I like him to feel good about himself, and that through me personally, through my actions, my little surprises, my wanting him, and my want-to-be with him. Men miss those little actions, they deserve to be loved, and for those who are waiting for men to take the first step, let me share with you, many will not. So, ladies, let's step out of our shell, take the initiative and take the lead. But what about women? Women are the easiest to love, the jacket that I was covered with day one, I will never forget, he got me back then, before he even rubbed my neck and shoulders. Was it easy to go? No. I simplified his life and mine, our life was complicated enough to walk on eggshells; as for the flower and the note, women love that. It was a pure romantic action, well appreciated and to be remembered forever; holding the hand, the touch, the whisper in the ear, all are actions that would make a woman melt in her man's arms. If loving a man is easy, and loving a woman is even easier, where is love, and why is it that loving our partner becomes so cumbersome after marriage?

To my love, the man who deserved my love, actions speak louder than words. A very famous statement that tells a simple story; do you remember why you decided to marry that woman, who just happen to co-live with you in the same house? Do you remember what you did on your second date? Well, the second date is more important than the first one, it is the one that decided on the third date and the ones coming after. Simple advice, if a woman accepted you then, it means she accepted you forever. Don't take her for granted, keep the flame lit, keep her heart on fire, remember to pinch her behind as she passes by, remember to comment on her dress even though it's not the first time she wore it, and remember to kiss the side of her lips occasionally. Remember to make her day every day, and mainly don't leave space for a man coming from the darkness to rock her world in her dream, or be her dream.

Chapter 12

Between the man in my dream and the man of my dreams, I started restoring my emotional stability, and that, by living two lives. On a professional level, I climbed the business ladder like shooting stars. I did not fail a task, and every task, to me, was a challenge and ended up with success. Working with the school principal was a personal development on its own. With my passion towards every task, I started spreading my wings throughout different departments at school. I started with him in March 2001, when he took leadership of the school. First tasks, the purchasing and financial departments, as for the first personal development, I had to understand the team spirit. That to me was the most challenging task, knowing my background and personality.

With time, I took charge of additional non-academic departments; transportation, food and beverages, students/faculty and staff members' well-being, cleanliness, health and safety, security, official documentation with the government and Ministry of Education, stocks/inventories and orders, school image, marketing, physical plant and maintenance, boarding, human resources and payroll, backup systems, natural resources, and communication systems. I started as a business services coordinator and ended up the business affairs director. Slowly, after I co-chaired the accreditation process in 2005, I headed the personal and social development department in 2007, and in 2008 I became the director of middle school. Every task and department, were crowned successfully, and saying home is where the heart is, the school became my home.

Around that time, my long-gone brother, moved back to Lebanon with his family, and not only had we a great time, but his wife, helped me taking care of my daughters during the long hours I spent at work. She was an excellent mom, and she played an excellent role with my daughters in that side of my life.

As for the school principal, I developed a beautiful friendship with him and his family, the other directors on the team, and a couple of the school community. My social life was back on track, and occasionally my husband took part. The stress in the house was on eggshells, but manageable; my intimate life with my husband was at risk. My brother and his family left for France in 2003, it was difficult for me losing them again, but by then I was used to farewells, and I was busy with my own life. In January 2006, we bought a house. Finally, the house of my dreams, and in my name. I started working on the house, and by July 2006, it was ready for us to move in. It was the starting day of the 2006 war in Lebanon. That morning I called the moving company, because they were late, the owner answered me saying that the whole business was attacked, including all the moving trucks. I was determined to move, fearing to take it as a negative sign, and especially because all was packed. I made some calls, arranged another moving company, and by the night we were installed. I told myself, a new fresh start with my husband, it will bring us a new spirit to the house, with a new aura. It was a beautiful house, four stories, a garden, and mainly my dream kitchen. That day started messy, being the superstitious person I was, I should have read the signs; the house was full of workers, Vanessa was in her room unpacking, Tiffany was on the patio playing on her roller blades, people were in and out, workers cleaning and helping. Suddenly, fighter jets were in the area, and the sound of the dropped bombs very near, I froze, I started calling the girls' names. Vanessa was up in her room, as for Tiffany, she ran to the door, it was locked and she couldn't come in. Her dad ran to her, opened the door, everyone was safe but, it was quite a disastrous moment. The bomb was dropped in the area of the building where the school principal resides, a dark cloud covered the whole area, and despite the sound of the bomb, silence took over for a while, then we started hearing the sirens of the ambulances. My husband went to check on them, they were safe. An hour later, the doorbell rang, I went to the door, it was him, the principal, my friend, coming to say goodbye; another farewell ... they were leaving the country, like many other families; there were no safe places. As for us, we stayed, with the emergency bag ready, going through the minutes and hours, one after the other, and one bomb after the other, it was a very stressful time. Our social life consisted of the area we lived in. Bridges were bombed, the traffic to and out of our area was horrible. Probably, I over panicked, but I was really scared. With the principal and his family leaving, and many others, I started thinking about what if they never came back? Would my life remain the same? Was it another goodbye cycle? No answers ...

The situation was very bad for the next couple months, people were anxious, nervous and out of control. I went to visit a friend with my daughters, her husband acted in a very inappropriate, unacceptable, harassing way ... I left and never was able to face my friend, or visit them again. I always discussed harassment with my students, it has always been a lecture till I experienced the real feeling. I was lonely, disgusted, intimidated, scared to be judged, or blamed, like any victim, and I was lucky I was able to block him; but in fact, he was a dirty, filthy and the low so-called friend. We were living under enough pressure to add another one, I tried to calm myself and forget the incident as much as possible.

The situation in the country was way more complicated than a personal one. With no other choice, and a bleeding soul, I moved on. My friend, the principal, was calling often to check on us and the school situation. His calls gave me hope and more appreciation of his friendship. The airport and exit borders were all almost closed, we had one last chance to leave. We were already in August, my husband and I had a discussion, and agreed to leave the country with the girls, in a week if the situation didn't get any better. Luckily, there were discussions for a permanent cease fire, and indeed it happened. With peace back to town, many people came back, and I started feeling life coming back to me. I put the harassment incident behind me, but never was able to forget the feeling, face my friend or her family. A couple months after, I grabbed the phone, called my friend's husband, told him all I thought of him, and the kind of person he was … I could not tell him I wish the same would happen to his three daughters, because I have girls of my own. I think he heard me well, he apologized, but it was like apologizing to a dead person after their death. Anyways, I survived with a scar, as for him, I was waiting for karma to pay back, and I knew the incident was his worst nightmare.

Somehow, incidents became my nurturing strength, I became the woman of many hats and lives.

2006 was a breaking point, I looked at my life from a different perspective. On a professional level, I couldn't be in a better position; on my daughters' level, they were adolescents and that made me wonder about my future; and on the marital level, we were partners in that institution. My daughters started going out in the early evenings, and here, I started going out to coffee shops, waiting for them to finish, and came back home all together. School events consisted of couple times during the year, and that was it. Still, I was a loner, I cannot say that I was miserable, but I wasn't happy. I started thinking about the separation more and more. I couldn't live without love, I had a lot to offer, so I indulged more with my dream, the man of my dreams, with whom I used to let go of myself in his arms and on his shoulder. My older daughter Vanessa was fourteen, and Tiffany was still too young, around eleven, which means they were still at risk of being hurt if separated from their father. Although I believed that children are stronger than we think, I couldn't take the risk. So back to my room, alone at night, with my thoughts and passion, I slept with tears in my eyes, and my heart aching for love. Did I not deserve passionate nights? A question I kept asking myself. So I kept myself busy with the house and garden. But after finally having the house I always wanted, it turned out that happiness never consisted of the walls and bricks surrounding us. My feelings were still the same, as in every house I lived in. Additionally, I started having stress symptoms. Back and forth to the doctor, with chest pain, unstable blood pressure, headaches, and breathing problems. I did all kinds of medical tests.

I thought I had a brain tumor, I did an MRI, it came out negative; I thought I had heart problems, I did the ECG and all was normal; the doctor recommended tranquilizers, but I refused to take any; I refused to put myself on treatment to enjoy my life.

I filled my weekdays at work, but when the working hours ended, I used to feel darkness, moreover, the nights were killing me, in small doses. I had no interests other than work, and I started wondering about the day the man I loved followed me to the States. Did I make a mistake sending him away? What would my life have been like? Did I allow my ego to stand in the way of my happiness? I was lost. All I had were the special moments I lived as a dream. I couldn't tell whether they were a dream or reality. I never wanted to end those moments, but at the end, I had to, I had to come back to reality. My dream of growing with my husband side by side was fading away. Did I lose my chance of happiness by not divorcing earlier? Well, it was too late to go back in time, so, I visited the priest one last time, to check if there were any other changes to my situation. The only solution was to break the family apart, and I couldn't. All the signs were negative, my health was deteriorating, and the depression was taking me down. I added more weight, which made me feel worst about myself. Except, the man in my dream, he never complained. He loved me as is, he saw the beautiful woman in me, and he cherished me. His friendship and passion were my stepping stones to sunshine in the darkest moments. Which made me wonder if my husband ever loved me. With him I enjoyed the woman I was, as with my husband, I used to be simply a wife. Was that the story of every woman? No, despite the ups and downs of marriage, the couple fought for each other, as for us, we lost all interest. Yet, I used to wonder whether it was my mistake. Partially, it was, but when I felt he had no interest in me, it blocked my feelings towards him, and I pursued passion elsewhere. Why didn't he wonder whether I was getting my passion fulfilled? To me, that was my answer. He didn't care, all he was concerned about was the house operation, and that made me his partner, and not his wife.

That year, Vanessa was graduating from high school with distinction, Tiffany passed to grade ten, and as I was dressing Vanessa in her distinction collar, my life flashed in front of my eyes. She went on stage for her valedictorian speech, she was radiant and glimmering, she had a successful and proud smile on her face. I looked at her dad, he was so happy and happy for her. At that moment, I realized that what I always told them was true. He had his own way of loving them, they were to love him and accept him as is, and mainly not to try and change him. At that moment, I was happy we were still together, despite the way I always felt. I was happy they grew alongside his presence despite all the empty moments we survived. Vanessa might never understand what I went through during my life with him, all I cared about, was the glow on her face, and whether it would have been there, if I had broken the house. I chose to marry him, and I had to be responsible for my decision. Probably he went through the same emptiness I did, but why didn't he do something about it? Probably, he did not know any better.

Towards his daughters, he was a good father, the father he knew how to be; towards me, we had our rare happy moments, but not enough memories for us to make us hold on to each other. Between sarcasm, demeaning attitudes, and neglect, I lost all attractions towards him, and I preferred not to be with him in public. Although I spoke out, he never changed, but did I ever act back in public? No, instead, I pulled myself back, and I rejected him. I rejected him, not only in public, but as well intimately. Probably, I wasn't the wife and woman he wanted, dreamt about, and looked for, but when he married me, I was the sociable, active, and working woman he claimed he loved, and more importantly, I was living abroad, alone, with my friends, in my own apartment, and I was the master of my own destiny.

Chapter 13

Happiness has always been within me, I always found a strategy to reach it, mainly I was always content with what I had, and never asked for the out of ordinary. All I ever wanted was a family. I loved to have girls and I was granted two. I wanted to own a house with a garden as a security for my senior age, and after sixteen years of marriage, I was granted a beautiful house. I wanted to build things from scratch with my partner, and I did. I wanted to be a successful business woman, and I was. I wanted a simple social life with my family, and here is where things did not come true. Since the 2006 war and on, my husband created his own social life with friends. His life consisted of gatherings over BBQs, playing soccer, basketball, and other activities away from us and throughout the days of the week. The social life he chose alienated me farther from him. None of us, myself or the girls, were happy with his choices but those were his choices, and not a subject for discussion. We were living apart from each other, under one roof, meeting occasionally with the couple friends we had. By then, I was confident that our life together had no future. On a personal level, I was more independent, and as for my daughters, Vanessa had already graduated, and Tiffany was in her senior school years. I had never discussed my life with my husband with the girls, therefore, all they knew, we were living separate lives. I never failed to fulfill my duties as a mom, and we were always very close, even to share their love life. But with both of them being close to eighteen, I was more secure in terms of the church law taking them away from me, in case we hit the divorce. Additionally, being financially well established, played a huge role towards my security. I know the relationship between the man and woman changes after marriage, but marriage is a unity between two people, and not an expectation of duties. Men and women have commitments towards each other; once those commitments filter down to becoming duties, the marriage becomes at risk. Our problem was not only related to passion, or love, it became lack of interest in the presence in each other's life. In the beginning, around 2006, I thought he was going through his mid-life crisis, concerned about his age, growing away from his partner, the girls growing etc. ... although, not a single time did he decide to go on a vacation and I stopped him. The change of path he chose, between friends and activities, he knew, it was not my style, and nor the girls. I had always told him, that being parents for girls, we needed the open door and trust policy for them to feel comfortable bringing their boyfriends home; but unfortunately, it was not his style. I was fully liberal when it came to my daughters' social life, and of course supervised and with limits, while he was very reserved. I always believed that our children outsmarted us parents, whatever they wanted to do during the evenings and nights out, they can easily do during the days. I have done it to my parents, like many other teenagers. I believed overprotecting our children could lead them to mistakes and disappointments. But this was not our main problem, our problem was strictly related to lack of interest in each other's way of life and life as it goes. With the girls growing, and him trusting me following them every step of the way, he wasn't present in that part of raising them. With me being an excellent financial manager of the house, he never felt the pressure to overwork in order to fulfill their needs. Things were smooth, and because of my position at work, I was able to ask for a small yearly bank loan in order to spoil them. Life was good in that side of life, but I was as well, a self-content woman. I had a female friend who used to tell me, for a man to work hard he has to always live under a financial pressure. It makes sense somehow, my husband never felt any financial pressure, and the girls' education was not paid for, since I was working at school. They were in a private international school, and the tuition fees were high compared to other private schools, but that was my choice and I went for it. My husband always knew, and expected the financial expenses due, within a margin; this was excellent for him as the man of the house, no major surprises, vacations, or unknown payments. I was on fire in terms of wanting more, working harder, and spending longer hours at work, while he used to wake later, and spend less hours at work. This bothered me a lot, and always worried me; it does not mean that I was the man of the house, he paid his share, from a business perspective. I want to clarify a point, for my husband to spend fewer hours at work, it does not mean he couldn't cover the expenses needed, but he never showed any intention to do more, give more, never planned anything together as a couple or family, I never asked for more, he mostly complained about the economic situation in town, and mainly he never reassured me of the future security. I was never a woman with a jealous character, but I used to wonder why he had no interest to create memories with me or his family. It is wrong, because what fixes a relation between a woman and her man, are the little moments they spend behind the scenes, away from their children, in public, a dance, a new song that got them to sink intimately, breakfast in bed, an invitation to dinner, a date to the movies, and anything that would make them wake up in the morning, look into each other's eyes, and have that flirty smile. I missed that, or rather I never recalled the last time it happened. I, on the other hand, used to feel like a woman, outside the house where I resided with him for 20 years as a partner. It is sad, it did break my heart, because when I used to encounter an older couple, feeding each other, or holding hands in public, I used to look at them with envy and tell myself, where did I flunk it up? For a while, I lost confidence in my physical attraction, I thought I had no more social skills, I felt that I did not know how to please a man … but wait, I was a sexy, attractive, and appealing woman, who never passed unseen, or unnoticed; I enjoy life, and myself, and I have skills; and I'm talking about the skills under the cover. Yes, I am proud of myself for being that kind of woman, the woman my husband met in the States, having a women's night out, enjoying her life, and mastering her own destiny. While you, the man that chose that woman, listen, my dear sweetheart, if you can't catch up with such a woman, don't take her and try to break her. A woman with natural skills, can give to you because she wants to, and not because you said so, and here I am not talking about the skills under the cover. Do you feel the anger in my words? Because right now, I am angry, and disappointed with myself for being angry, I just want to be selfish now. I do not want to think about my daughters, I do not want to regret any achievement I have accomplished, I want to talk about the woman inside me. Where were her rights to be loved and treated with passion? Who took care of her during the heated thoughts and nights? Where was the man who married her and forgot her, who was waiting for her when she walked down the aisle, who was decorating the church for her with his own hands, and had to rush home and get ready? Why did he let go after marriage and lose interest in her?

Well, all I can say, he was not there. As for me, I stopped caring. I was done: marriage became a duty, and a duty towards my daughters. The beautiful dream house I always wanted felt like a one room jail. My girls were on their way to fulfill their own destination, and me, my sentenced years were close to an end. I used to look at the beautiful house and see just walls … and I knew then, I was done. My heart was aching for the twenty years of my life that were wasted, it was not only love I wanted, it was not only passionate moments I cried for, it was rather and in addition to that, not having my husband part of the memories we lived as a couple and a family. He was not part of the memories at the daily dinner table, morning coffee, movies, evenings, gatherings … where did I fail and why?

It was January 2010, my husband's fiftieth birthday, Tiffany's fifteenth birthday and mainly our twentieth anniversary. I decided to celebrate, it was due, and at least to me, I always cherished every event, and was so excited. So I told him that I was preparing a dinner to avoid surprises with him. I contacted my family, his family, some couples, Tiffany's friends and their parents, some of Vanessa's friends, I got a one man show, I prepared the whole meal myself, and that saying that I was working full time. It was so beautiful, I don't remember how I generated the energy to fix the whole thing, but I'm sure most of the energy was related to celebrating Tiffany's birthday. Anyway, the house was busy with the preparations, the kitchen was over packed with baking and cooking dishes, the one man show was setting up his corner and testing the sound system etc. ... my husband came in! He saw the preparations, asked who was coming, we had our fight, I was disappointed, he was upset, but, of course, nothing changed. I was used to that, I was even used to him not being emotionally ready for the visitors, if ever anyone would come. But what really hurt me most, was that I was part of that celebration, and probably he should have considered surprising me. Anyway, they all came, the event was a huge success, everyone was happy, well seated, comfortable, food was excellent, and he was actually happy, a good host, smiling, laughing ... oh, oh, oh, how much I ached for those moments, why you never granted them to me. With all the happiness in my heart looking at the full busy house, giggling walls, laughing faces and singing atmosphere, I knew all that would not go beyond that evening.

Indeed, it was a day to remember, and the only one. I received many calls the next day, mentioning the hosting, and good times. Soon after, the water channeled back into its stream; the routine took over again; and the worst thing in life that could ever happen to a person, is sensing the taste of happiness, and most importantly, knowing that the other half within the couple is capable of being sociable and bringing the good times in. At that point my anger towards him started growing. I couldn't forgive him, I couldn't tell whether he pushed me away or we let go of each other, all I knew, I was already gone. With frustration, I faced the upcoming days. The evening that brought happiness to me that day, was my wake up call. I always read signs around me, and that was my sign. He did not care about my feelings, my well-being, and what I wanted. He was content with himself, his life, and his own lifestyle. As for me, now, I wanted more and on all levels. I was ready to move on.

It was the beginning of the summer, time to relax and enjoy the sun, the girls got busy with different plans, many of their friends traveled and others were here, again, routine on the go, days in and days out, I looked around, and as I usually do every summer, I evaluated my life. With all my success in sight, I was not happy, satisfied, or pleased with my life. It was Saturday, I invited a couple over to lunch, they were his friends as well, and it was not the first time they had come over. Suddenly, we started fighting over a silly matter, it went out of control, it was the cherry on the pie. I asked him not to repeat what he just did, and in my heart I told him that he would pay for it dearly. I went back down to my guests, and discretely I asked them to leave shortly. The fight we had was the drop of water that flooded the cup, for one reason or another. He felt that he could empty the house fully from all friends because he just wanted to go play soccer at his own ease, well, what he did not know, was that the couple were close enough for me to ask them to leave the house, but mainly, I was planning my way out.

    I took a couple days alone, thinking about myself, and shuffling my life events in my mind, asking myself about the evenings I spent alone for years, while other women were out, having fun or cuddling with their partners, wondering whether I was ready or not, to set the freedom path to myself. And like the thunders in summer days, it struck me that it was time to move on, and start taking care of myself.

Chapter 14

It took me around a week of tears, isolating myself, thinking about the next step. I called my friends, the ones I had asked to leave during my fight with my husband, explained the situation and apologized. But they were not anymore my concern, I was thinking about the girls and the steps to follow. So, the next Saturday morning I went down to our church, my family church, I went to the grave where my birth mother and father were resting. I stood in front of the grave; I couldn't pray, instead, I burst into tears, complained to my father for allowing the ghosts to hurt me, him, my brother, my sister, for him letting things happen, then I told both of them, get up, I never asked for help from you both, ever in my life, it is time to play your role, and stand by me. I went to the priest, I hugged him, asked him to come and pray for them, which he did. Then, we went into his office, I announced to him that I was ready to file for divorce. He wondered why we were still together, he asked about my daughters' ages, and the main reason behind the divorce. Based on the information I gave, he said that both girls would have to testify in court; that our church law would grant me the divorce after three years in my case, a detail he failed to mention to me in the past; while we were living separate lives for around eleven and a half years so far; that I would need a very knowledgeable lawyer, and he gave me couple contacts and told me that it would be costly. My answer was, I had enough jewelry to buy my freedom. I went back home with my contacts, and slept through a couple of nights for a decision to form. Meanwhile, in the afternoon, I opened Facebook, to see an inbox message. I opened it: it was from the love I always wondered about. I said, "Who is this?" the reply was, "Are you the love of my life, and the person I lost and hurt the most?" It was him. Did fate send me strength to go on, a sign? To me, that is what it was. We started chatting, he told me he was divorced, he had three daughters, and we started chatting again. Having him back in my life gave me hope, and he being divorced gave me strength.

Throughout the years of marriage, remember, I was away from praying and church for years, since the day I lost my sister. So Sunday morning, I drove early to Saint Charbel, I went to the area where he used to sit and talk to God. I sat there for hours, cried my heart out, and told him my story. I asked him to give me strength, to ask for divorce. On my way back, my husband called me, asking where I was, I told him and he sarcastically answered, you are becoming a saint. I reached home, lit the candle I bought from Saint Charbel. I sprayed the house with the essence I bought from the monastery there, I woke the girls up, got them ready, and went to lunch with them with the intention to discuss the divorce. During lunch, I informed them about the past two days, and my intentions. They were both very supportive, saying that anyway we lived separate lives, and that I deserved to have a happy life. Additionally, they mentioned how the mothers of their friends lived a life I never had. Then I told them that this was my plan since they were very young, but fearing of losing their custody in court, because this was the church law of our religion, I waited till they were old enough; but since they were both under eighteen, they would have to stand in court and testify, and say who they would wish to live with. Vanessa was close to eighteen then, so Tiffany, fifteen and a half, said, I will do the talking, but make sure I go with you. She loved her father dearly, but she was closer to me. I told her, for whatever it takes, I will not proceed if I cannot secure your custody, and even both your custody. Somehow, my husband felt that I was different the past week, different than any prior time we fought in the past, so he called while we were having lunch, and we started fighting. I told him I would see him in the early evening, we wrapped our lunch, and I went home. I asked the girls to leave and go see their friends. I went inside the house, he was drinking, hysterical, and he had the bible in front of him. I was scared, I was shivering, I started praying in my heart, for

Saint Charbel to give me the strength I needed. He asked me to sit by him, I refused, I told him the big news, while my voice was failing to be heard, and blood was failing to flow in my veins, I looked at him and said, "I want the divorce."

Again, the same story, I will take the girls away from you, he said, and will drag you to court for years. My answer was, "If I die one day free and away from you, I will fight you in court, and let the church decide." Days passed, I started losing weight from fear, and developed sleep apnea. The doctor I visited, the one who knew my history with my husband, recommended a ventilator during my apnea attacks. A friend of mine, at school, a speech therapist, gave me strength, by saying, I don't care about the reason that made you develop sleep apnea, you are a strong woman, using the ventilator, will help you breathe, but will weaken your vocal cords, and I would have to work on you next. She said, you are a symbol of strength for us all, be the woman you are. I minimized the use of the ventilator, except for emergencies, and went on with the days, determined to succeed, and reach my new goal, freedom. He wanted me to swear on the bible, that I had never cheated on him, I did swear, but what about the man of my dreams, and the man in my dream. Anyways, it did not matter to me, because God was already not appreciative of me breaking the oath I took in church, the day I said I do. But Dear God, did you not remember the oath he had given me? The promises of a man to his woman, to stand by his wife in richer and in poorer, in sickness and in pain, and till death took us apart. Where was he when I had my gallbladder full of stones attack at night, and when I woke him up, he asked me to take pain killer pills. I had to drive myself to the hospital, at one after midnight. So I called a friend of mine, who stayed with me on the phone while I almost fainted from pain, she met me in the hospital, and stayed with me till the early hours of dawn. I was supposed to stay till the next morning for additional tests, but I just wanted to go back home and send my daughters myself to school. I did not want the girls to wake up and not find me there. When the pain soothed, my friend drove me home. When I got home, my husband was deep asleep in his room. Where was his oath, during many similar incidents? Well, I had a lot to discuss with God, with my husband, and the judge in court. I had no more fear and the weakness I survived throughout the twenty years of marriage, turned into audacity and strength. I was facing a war, and I had nothing to hide, or shame in my life. No one knew about the divorce, other than my friend the school principal, and one of the directors with whom I had a very close friendship. One day, I received a call from her husband, asking me to meet him, his wife the director, and my friend the principal, and that the meeting was requested by my husband. So we did, we met in a coffee shop, they informed me of the reason behind the meeting, but prior to leaving, my husband had asked me to calm down and listen to them. I already knew that there were promises of change, but it was too late for me. I briefly told them, after listening to them about my life with my husband, and I announced to them that my decision was final. I went back home, my heart was broken, not because of the meeting, but because of the time he ignored me, and he knew he was doing so. The decision was very difficult, painful, and hard on me, but my health and happiness were my priority, and I would be no good to my daughters, if sick and helpless. I used to look at my daughters after they slept, crying and hoping for their understanding and forgiveness, and for the first time after years, I started praying for strength from above, and thanking God, for all the strength, and the times he carried me during my helpless moments, despite the fact that I was angry at him and with unanswered questions. During that time, I requested of both my best friends, the principal and the director, to keep my divorce unannounced, and chose the side they would like to support and stand by. Meanwhile, I went and saw my long lost love. With an affectionate hug we received each other, and never went beyond that hug; seeing him brought only the good times back to surface. I used to meet him after work in a coffee shop, where we both sat on different tables and chatted through Facebook. Then I would go home to my daughters, where they were worried, but not showing it, and I would do the same. Every evening after that, my husband would call me to go down to him and chat. Some evening discussions were tough, others were just getting to know each other, what we should have done early in the marriage and not after twenty years. Before I went down to him every night, Tiffany would tell me, stay strong, I am here for you. Golden supportive words from a fifteen-year-old, but this is life. I apologized daily for the tension she was living, asking God to give them both the strength to move on. Sadly, twenty years of marriage went to toss, because of neglect and ignorance. I realized one night, and through our chat, that the woman of his dreams, was not my style of woman, he preferred a classical housewife, and not a working and liberal woman. I knew as well, during those evening discussions about his first love, the challenges he was faced with throughout our life, he learned then about my life with the ghosts, my birthday date, what I like and dislike. We lived among those nights some laughs and conversations we both regretted not having. Why did we break a family, why were we traumatizing our daughters and ourselves? Didn't we have enough love to build our family, our future and maintain a relationship that would last us together forever? We did, we both did, we were both lost. I had many after thoughts, but mainly I could not get over the pain deep inside of me. Among the conversations, and long evenings we spent chatting, we went through ups and downs, some evenings were just the exchange of thoughts and others were heated with threatening discussions. I did let the wolves out with my decision but I couldn't withdraw, and not for egoistical reasons. I was convinced that it was too late to launch a reconciling phase. Days after, I started the search for a lawyer, after days and different meetings, I decided on one. I was convinced that I was alone and I did not want to drag anyone in either the search or the decision. I did not even inform my own family about the situation. Partially, I did not want any conflicts between them and the father of my children. Eventually, they were to meet in different occasions, and he was going to be there against all odds, simply because I was divorcing him myself; I had not planned to get him out of my daughters' life, he had the right to be their father and they had the right to have him as a father, and to choose, based on the after-divorce, how much they wanted him in their lives. The other reason behind not informing my parents was related to the closeness we had, we were close but not close enough. I never knew how they would react, whether they will stand by me and my decision, or choose to get us back together. It was my decision, my war, and my war with my husband, privately and not publically. I withdrew from close friends slowly, in order to avoid any confrontations between my husband and family members or friends. The only confrontation we had, was between the two of us. All I wanted was a peaceful divorce, hoping to cause the least damage possible to all four of us, myself, my daughters and my husband. Finally, I decided on a lawyer, I went to him and I started informing him about my story. Again I heard the same thing; the church law stated that any time a husband and wife live separate lives for a period exceeding three years, the church grants the divorce based on that reason. Additionally, both daughters will be called to court, despite their age, and mainly, the lawyer said that we should be tough enough to face each other at a specified time, because once we get close to divorce, gossip and stories will be invented to delay the decision of the judge. This would be deteriorating and degrading to both of us, since we both would want to exit victorious. The lawyer, after discussing with me all the steps of the church divorce, and the time needed to receive it, which is a minimum of three years in case we do not agree on the divorce and the terms of the divorce, asked me to think things over for a couple of days and bring him the official marriage records. The marriage records were not a problem, I had them in a briefcase in my room throughout the twenty years of marriage. As such, I went home, took some time to think, a time I never needed, yet, the issue of taking the girls to court and degrading each other was my main concern. Anyway, decision set, I took the content of the briefcase to the lawyer, in order to check the documents and follow through, and to my surprise, it turned out that when my husband sent our marriage documents in the States to be officially recorded, he sent the court marriage and not the church marriage!

Twenty years of waiting, fearing he would take away my daughters in a church divorce were not applicable in my case, I could have been set free a long time ago based on the court marriage law ... but, should I have any regrets?

Chapter 15

As I was discussing the divorce with my husband one night, and he was aggravating the idea and situation, I informed him about the court records and he went crazy. He requested to see the papers; I told him they were already with the lawyer. At that point, he realized I was serious and the decision was final. The next days were very intense and the conversations we had were even harsher. My goal was to reach a communicative level, in order for him to understand that I did not want any degrading separation. After all, we had two girls we needed to raise together, and all I ever wanted was my freedom. I understood the way he was feeling and reacting, first, he was not expecting me to ask for the divorce, he thought like my prior fights, he could upset me and I'd try to fix the situation; he thought, after me requesting the divorce, he could threaten me by taking away my daughters, but it was no longer the case, because he had registered the court and not the church marriage; and last, he was shocked with my determination and thought I had someone supporting me, while I was totally alone.

The divorce phase was very difficult, especially as it was the beginning of the school year. I had to be in a perfect shape emotionally and physically fit. I had requested of my friends that the divorce remain private at least till it was done, but of course, anytime a secret went beyond one person, it was no longer private and a secret. Everyone at school was congratulating me for losing weight, while many knew, they respected my privacy, I used to answer by saying I went on a severe diet. The school year launched beautifully, that was one of my strengths, to separate personal from professional. I used to meet with the lawyer after school hours in order to avoid any disruption at school. As I was going through the process alone, my husband had some friends helping him and teaching him what to do. We never spoke during the day; our meetings took place during the evenings. Although I was very weak, scared, and falling apart, I couldn't let my feelings be visible to anyone, and especially not to my daughters. Therefore I stood my ground and remained focused. The lawyer was pushing me to come to an understanding with my husband in order to rush the process. I remained calm during all our conversations, and I used all the conflict resolution techniques and skills I used to teach my students at school. Nevertheless, there were times when I cried begging my husband to let me go. I was too tired to go on with the marriage, moreover, I was disappointed with the outcome. My husband was in denial of our situation, at least to me. I couldn't understand how a man would accept not having a social and/or close life with his wife. Let's say he fulfilled that part of his life, I'm sure he did because I was told so, but it was a one night stand relationship, at least those were my feelings, and similar to any other married man; but wouldn't he wonder how his wife was handling herself, or who was taking care of her for years? Why is it that he accepted the situation for a while, and then suddenly he questioned it? The answer was obvious, he had his needs fulfilled, and had no more interest in me. During the process, he tried to win me back, but unfortunately, I was no longer interested in him, he was a total stranger. The worst day was the day he promised me that he would have the open door policy for my friends, he would be a good host, and would grant me the social life I always wanted. At that time, I just wanted to slap him, and choke him; I was silent and speechless, the whole twenty years flashed in front of my eyes, my mind was numb, my thoughts were dispersed all over ... it hit me, that he was aware of what I wanted, and what was the norm in a couple's life, yet, he chose to drop our social life and my life with him; I looked at him, no, it was not the death look, it was rather the too late look, and that was my exact answer, too late. I explained to him that we no longer loved each other, cared for each other, or asked about each other; he deserved a woman that would love him the way he wanted, I was too passionate while he was looking for just love, and not sure that he was looking. Honestly, after twenty years with him, I never knew what he liked. Till the girls were grown-ups, he forgot most of my birthdays, and the holidays meant nothing to him. He did not even believe in Santa Claus, don't laugh, yes I do, and till today, and it's the spirit of Christmas. Anyways, I was done, ready to move on, and I wanted two things, my freedom and the custody of my daughters. He is what we call a good guy, but not my guy. Between the ups and downs, and hours of negotiations, finally, we reached a verdict. I got the girls' custody, and a financial settlement, while he got the house.

The divorce was settled with the minimal damage possible. Although a family was broken, and I knew nothing about the future, I just wanted my freedom, and I wanted to go to a home at night with no pressure. I took off only one day from school, for it was the judgment day. It was a Friday, we stood in front of the judge for around three seconds, where he asked us whether we both agreed to terminate our partnership, we answered positively, and that was it.

Twenty years ended in seconds, sadly, and why? It was heartbreaking, we shook hands, I couldn't look him in the eyes, and each went our own way. I couldn't go back to school, although that was the plan. I just went and sat alone in a coffee shop for hours.

I called my step-mother, informed her that I wanted to see her on Saturday morning. I went to her, I told her the shocking news. With the end in sight, I gave her the details. The first Monday after the divorce, I went to school, and I received more congratulations and salutes than the day I married. I was told, my action spoke on behalf of many women who never dared to act, and I was envied for my courage and the step I took.

Twenty years ago, I took a decision to marry. It was rushed, within a few months of the meeting day, we were married. And today, within a few months of my decision to divorce, we were single again, and I mean on paper. Human being's decisions are weird, and at least, I'm talking about myself. Whenever I decided to do something, I moved with it. I never took the time to analyze the pros and cons. I always believed that the time invested on the thinking, took away from the time needed for development.

The aftermath phase ... I was on a go! I could not express my feelings, whether excited about the new house, happy with my freedom, or agitated with the preparation of the move, I felt emptiness and silence within me. Friends were around me, supporting me, and my social life got busier ... yet, I guess the speed of the events did not give me time to adjust and balance. Some days were good, others were bad, and as time went by, I started feeling emotionally tired. I tried to keep busy with Christmas coming, and New Year, but time was still. Moving forward was heavy, especially if we carried the debris of the past along to the future. Furthermore, I could not detach myself from my husband. Although I wanted the divorce, I kept on worrying about him, what he was doing, his plans for the holidays, etc. ... at the end of the day, he was my partner for twenty years, and I couldn't but wish him happiness and health. My daughters got well settled under the new roof, and although the house was way smaller in size than the house with their father, we were happy. In the beginning, we had a schedule for the girls to spend time with their father and at their father's house, as for me and him, communication was heated for a long while. I never used our daughters in any occasion or holiday, as a fighting tool, instead both of us, myself and my ex, made sure the girls attended every celebration with both families; I never manipulated their feelings into the favorite parent game; and mainly I wanted to make sure they understood that I divorced him myself and not them. I never knew that I would worry about him this way after the divorce, I even thought about him more than I ever did. At times, I used to become angry at him for wasting my twenty years, but then again, I had no one to blame but myself, no one hurt us without our consent, and our consent means simply silence. Words are the only precious weapon, when used, but when disappointments take over our spirit, we lose interest, faith, and trust, in self, and in others. My emotions became very unstable, my thoughts were scattered everywhere, yet, I was still functioning properly with matters related to my professional life and daughters.

My first breakthrough after the divorce was me connecting with the long lost love I always thought about. I don't know whether it was a mistake, but it did end within three months and left me with financial damages. We enjoyed discussing the past more than we did living the present, and to my surprise, before I left for the States, we took pictures on the staircase of the building, pictures that were never developed. So I found in my memory box the negatives, I developed them, and they brought to surface the good times we had before the sad ending. We spent some good times together, but I guess it was not enough for us to survive a long sleeping love. At least, I rested my case in terms of thinking about him, and wondering how life would have been with him. I guess what was not meant to be, shall never happen. Anyway, it was part of a past that hurt me in my early twenties, and was due to rest in peace. My trust in the human race was fading away. Was I weak and longing for love, so much that I did not know again who to be with or where to draw the line? Unanswered questions left me more lost than ever with fear to commit to others. What do men want, what are they looking for? But the main question I was reluctant to ask myself was what am I looking for? I believe I was supposed to terminate a past, with all its components, before I launched again. I had to stop giving from the heart, I had to stop loving passionately, I had to be wiser, and stop being impulsive … many characteristics that were within my character, and tough to let go of, or change. Honestly, I was not willing to change for anyone, it was my passion that made me survive and succeed, and it was through passion that I dreamt of the fairytale ending. During my downfalls, I cried my heart out for injuries that led me there, but during my upper rising phases, I used one sentence: tomorrow is a better day. I always managed to rise up and stand alone, and would not let the damaged recent nor old past keep me down. I always managed to find the rainbow of the rainy days and was convinced that success is within my reach. Teaching Peace Education at school, and seeing how much I was able to reach the students' souls and make them overcome their difficulties, made me the other woman. The woman who believed in change, and through personal convictions, rose. Nothing shall take me down forever, and mainly I will not allow myself to drag in a muddy situation.

So next, to better days, and to the future, a future that I will make for myself, and of myself. The only person that can help us, is ourselves. We, women, are born to handle the most challenging situations, and I was born to stand tall, because I was, am, and always will be the master of my own destiny.

Chapter 16

I was never a loner, and never was able to survive alone; when the reality blocked me, I started dreaming; and when the nights held me back, I extended the hours of the day to never sleep. I was a dreamer, full of life and a happy person by nature, despite all incidents. So, on the go again to connect with a man I met; he had just moved into the country and was planning his divorce. He fulfilled every dream I ever had, we lived the fairytale I always believed in, and spent together a time that made me emotionally strong. Where was he all my life, and what took him so long to show up? I guess it was planned to happen now and destined to pick me up and move on. This man got me wondering whether I ever knew what I wanted. I guess with time, age, and depending on circumstances, people think differently. Although before I met him, I was where I saw myself in my teenage years: a successful business woman, single, and with kids, but his passion towards life, and us sharing the same views related to spirituality, individual happiness, and humanity, made us soulmates. Indeed, he was my soulmate.

Did you ever wonder what your life would have been if you had not connected with the specific person you are with? Did you ever think about those you encountered throughout growing and made you who you are today? Did you believe destiny is IT? Well, I believe that destiny plays a role in our life, but when we let go of our dreams and passion for what we like, at this time we become dependent on our destiny, and stop dreaming. I believe our dreams are the only reality, chasing them keeps us alive. Probably, it is my active side, and my passion towards change that makes me think this way.

Well, I never thought I would end up in the education sector, but through this sector, I kept my business side, and developed my potential and creativity to succeed. I always loved kids, so I connected with them, and through character and peace education, I helped them change to their best. This means the frame was my destiny, but the content became my dream. It just happened that destiny put us in different places, locations, with different people, but our dream to achieve personal goals did not change, or stop, just because we were not there. And mainly, I did not allow the past to hold me back, instead, I used it as bouncing energy to lift me up. The heavier the past or current events were, the stronger the bounce was. That was my strength, a strategy I learned early in life, and it never failed me. The path was at times very harsh, but never blocked my dreams. Life is about determination, and the will to live, and survive. Find it inside your soul, it is there, don't let anyone put you down, don't let circumstances hold you back; use all your inner potential to prove the world wrong, and use your wisdom to reach your potential. You were born with a mission, manipulate your destiny to reach it. Develop yourself to become a leader, and not a follower. Let the world feel your existence, and let the people around you notice your achievements. Your goal is as big as your dream, and bigger than your current situation, even if you are happy, content, and satisfied. You will never know what's in Paris till you visit Paris, as well, if you hate Hitler, it does not mean you cannot go to Germany. Build your dream in your mind, live it through your imagination, and let the universe bring it to your reach. Those with no dreams shall live dormant, and die with regret. Time passes faster than the speed of light, if you fail to try the change early, you may not have the time to see it flourish. We love many times in life, those we loved at fifteen, we laugh at ourselves for loving them at twenty, but don't regret your actions, don't regret a past that changed you, a hand that slapped you, and another person that abused you. Don't blame them for their actions, for they were ignorant that they were the reason for you to bounce. Your success is relevant to your determination, and only those who dare to dream, shall live to see the other side of the main frame they lived, so-called their destiny. When those who hurt you, held you back, and demeaned you, when they realized that they were the strength you used to shine, and overcome them, it is then that they will realize their own failure, no matter how successful they would become. Your success was, is and shall be their weak point every time they look in the mirror; and how many times does one look in the mirror? Your success shall be their nightmare as they are awake more than during their sleeping time.

Therefore, every morning when you wake up, close your eyes, and see yourself accomplishing something new; look at yourself in the mirror, and tell yourself you are beautiful; live up to your potential, and walk tall, regardless of who put you down; you are what you make of yourself, your happiness is revealed through your smile, and your assertiveness is revealed through your body language. Barbie is a doll, it is the imaginary beauty of her creator; be the Barbie in your own eyes, and you shall reveal it to others. Size perfection is not in size, height, and weight, it is in the eyes of the beholder. If sizes were meant to be standardized, we would have been created in a pattern format, yet, each one of us women looks different, and even those born identical twins. Our physical appearance is not our only strength, we were born to talk, think and feel; and here is where the trick is. Those who are attracted to our physical appearance, would they look elsewhere when we change? And how about those who used their appearance to succeed, will they fail or stop developing when they change or age?

Success is reached through a combination of components, only some require physical beauty and specific sizes. Even though some might have features related to weight, heights, etc. ... that are required for the task or job, it does not mean that they are all capable of succeeding based on their physical beauty; and mainly, no success is commemorated without a thinking mind, a beautiful soul, and a caring and passionate heart longing for success.

Whether you are a working woman or a housewife, find your weakest point on which build your strength to reach happiness. Although women were born with a sensitive and emotional side, that would make them fall apart faster than men, and that is a general statement, remember that it is our sensitive and emotional side that will help us conquer and rock the world.

If you chose to be a non-working woman, and can afford it, whether through marriage or parental inheritance, live up to reveal your inner beauty, and allow no man, or other human to intimidate you, put you down, and make you feel any less important or precious. See yourself as a rare jewel, shine, in the darkness, in the light, and be your own star, before you become someone else's. Others may help you reveal the inside of you, but they did not make you, and therefore they did not own you. You are not a market piece, you are not the shadow of a man, and you are not his achievement; you are his frame, his sun, and his heart; you are the energy he needs to launch his day, and the pillow he needs to rest his case on last before he sleeps; you are not a punching bag, nor are you his intimate frustration release; instead you are the intimate unity that merges two powers into one to release the daily stress and boost positive emotions that can erupt like volcanoes of love, passion and desires. Women are granted with that power, so use it, and don't let it use you, and I am talking about emotions, not the other intimate powers, don't go far, use them to reach happiness and success.

If you are one of the women who chose a career, use all the skills you have to solve the business equation. If you are just a nine to five job person, and that makes you happy, do it with full passion, mind and soul. If you are a woman who becomes her job, do it with full passion, mind and soul. Success towards the public is not related to how far you go, it is based on how you reveal yourself; success toward yourself is revealed with how much you achieve of your dream through your own potential.

Don't let colleagues at work see your weakness or feel your fear. Conquer this world with self-confidence and trust, remember that you create your own image, and you reveal your own education. Degrees don't make people carrying them educated, it is the skills they reach through experience that reveals how educated they become. It does not mean I do not appreciate the degree carriers and their hard work pursuing their degree, but those who do not develop their personality, and show self-growth, their degree shall remain ink on paper. Don't let any higher authority keep you hidden, in the dark, and take away your credits … demand what you deserve, and set your own price; if you don't try, you will never know your worth in the eyes of the community you live in. It is important to strike through walls to exist, but don't remain in the wreckage you create. Use them to climb to a higher point, and remember the cost of every step. Usually, it is rare to reach success and high achievements in our life, except at the cost of other points, as high achievements require additional time and energy no matter how organized we could be. We may be able to balance our life and priorities in order to reach our goal, but as it shall never be enough, the support of our partner is highly needed. Women who decide to be the job, and reach it, while maintaining their social life, married life, and in some cases are mothers, they need their partners by their side, and positively, in order to reach their goals. Remember to create a balance that will allow you to enjoy both ends; no one should decide on how far you want to go, remember what lasts longer, and make sure you have a long-term vision. Discuss your vision with your partner and have it as a joint journey; if you fail to join your journey with your partner's, you might risk taking it alone … in simple terms, if you know what you want, and you are sure of your partner's point of view, whether in your favor or not, have the heart to proceed, for you do not want to reach a point of regret in life, where you look back and say, I wish I did. The support of the partner for a working woman, is a radical point in her success, not only because she might bring an extra penny home, but because her main success resides in the eyes of her partner. Women do need to feel appreciated for their efforts, and here I am talking about working and non-working ones alike, they need to be asked at the end of the day about their day as they ask their partner, what they did, what they ate, what they faced, and again working and non-working ones. When women are not appreciated for their efforts, they shall fail to regenerate strength in order to be happy and satisfy their partners, on a personal, intimate and professional level. And that was the appreciation I received from the man who knocked my door last;

he used to admire my potential to reach my goals; he believed in me, before I even saw my own strength; he saw the beauty of my soul, he saw the woman inside me; and therefore he pushed me to reach new skies ... His love, appreciation, and passion towards me, truly made me feel a new woman. I did reach higher skies with him, and we both celebrated the achievements together.

But as I always believed, the deeper and heavier the downfall is, the stronger the bounce is to rise; I also believed that the higher skies we reached, the deeper the fall would be, to leave us lost in a space without gravity to pull us back, and especially when we depended on our partners.

After reaching the point of happiness, I started feeling emptiness penetrating slowly like dark fog through every opening around me, and one day he came to me to reassure my feelings, telling me he was going back home. I guess happiness has a price, and the cost was called trust. Alone I was again, but this time, I was down, deep and hurt, and I guess with age, wounds don't heal quickly!

Chapter 17

Sadly, and more than ever, I found myself alone again, but this time, I isolated myself among a crowd. I lost trust fully in every human being. After my emotional crash, I looked at my life, I was surrounded by emptiness and silence. I used to look at people talking and say what kind of lies they were promising each other. Is that what people do, building imaginary castles for others, knowing they cannot fulfill their commitments? How can someone's personal interest take place at the expense of others? Anyways, again, I had to be strong for myself, to stand for myself, and move on. But one thing I could not ignore, was a true love, I truly believed that he was honest with his love; mainly, I guess I was not destined to find this true love, I was not destined to be with him.

Meanwhile, my family encouraged me to swap jobs, their dream was to bring the family together ... and deep inside I wanted to have them around me. We built reveries together, and I felt it was due for me and my daughters, to gather around a family during birthdays, christening, Christmas, etc. ... I put the ghosts of the past outside my life, I locked them away, far enough not to emerge again.

So leaving my sixteen years of school business was worse than my divorce. I trained many individuals to take over. My main concern was to ensure their success and not have them fail. This empire, the school, was my home, my own success, and the dream I saw arising, one step at a time. With tears and broken heart I let it go, hoping to find my own destiny through a new path, a different era.

July 31, 2013, I closed the door of my office, I locked sixteen years of past behind, but could not remove it from my heart. It was the same feeling I had when they threatened to take away my daughters from me. School was my baby, my growing child and my pride. Yet, I left for a new journey, I went to work with the family. I started the next day, but every day, I had tears in my heart, and on my cheeks. It was the divorce I never mourned, or got over. I couldn't survive, I thought it was a phase, but the feeling got worse with time.

Mid-August, on a summer evening, I was sitting on the house balcony with Tiffany; she was bored. I decided to give her the late eighteenth birthday present, a ticket to Paris. She was thrilled, she packed, and I arranged for her trip with my brother's wife, who was residing in Paris and made of the trip, a point of change in Tiffany's life. Tiffany, after spending the time of her life in Paris, announced to me after her ten days' vacation, that she was planning on pursuing her education abroad. A point of shock to me, I couldn't live with her away from me. But she got her dad's consent and blessing, and unfortunately, I could not get her mind out of the idea, especially with her dad by her side. The event ran very quickly, since her university in Paris started mid-September. I had no choice but to go with the flow.

We registered her, packed, and with a broken heart, I escorted her to her new journey. On the plane, I prayed for Mother Mary, telling her, she is a mother, she was the one who stood by me during my tough pregnancy with Tiffany, she was the one who helped me back then, and if she believed that this would be for Tiffany's best, I would accept her blessing, otherwise, to bring her back to me. The trip made me realize again, how attached I was to my daughters, and how much a family means to me. I wondered whether I was selfish with my prayers, but I left it in the hands of our Mother Mary, the mother of all. No one could be a better judge, but me, as the mother of Tiffany, I believed that she was too young for her independence, and she could still go for her masters in a couple years. Anyways, we went, but I guess the judgment of the mother of all, was by my side, and Tiffany came back with me. I know she did not favor or appreciate my decision, but it was too quick, and I'm convinced she was young.

So back to Lebanon we came, to face another dilemma, my work. I tried to adjust, and shift my mind off school. The principal, my friend, knew what I was going through. He tried to encourage me, and stood by me, but he could not understand the seriousness of the situation. My health started degrading again, headaches, blood pressure, and breathing problems, similar to the ones that happened during the last years of marriage and divorce. Yet, I stayed, and worked on myself. During that phase, I met a younger person, he kept me busy, and he was different than anyone I met in the past. I fell in love with him, but was hooked to a recent past that left me to go back home. Shortly after, I received an email, and a surprise visit. My fairytale love came back determined to be with me. Should I let go of a recent new young love? I still had feelings for him, I guess one does not learn from their own mistakes when it comes to the heart, so I left the young love, to go back to a love that hurt me.

And not only once, back and forth twice, with every jump call, I jumped, and every time higher than the previous time. How many times does a person make the same mistake? Was it a sign for me to understand that it was not meant to be, or was it a sign for me to understand that I should wait for him, till he was ready and capable to commit and stand by his words? An undetermined destined love, that, in my heart I believed was true, but in my mind I knew he could not let go of his own life. Well, I guess time will tell, but today, not only I am not with him, but I have been manipulating a younger soul who is accepting my situation and kept on waiting, insisting that one day I will wise up and be his, and only his, although repeatedly advised of my opinion about his age and my situation of trust.

My lack of trust in men made me torture the young love, yet all he saw in me was my beautiful soul and a heart that was manipulated. Was my heart manipulated or was I truly loved by someone who could not let go of me? How is it that every time I connected with someone else, fairytale love showed up to ask me to jump? To me, and because I believed in true love, I believed it was the universe that called him. I always believed that true love brings people together across the universe, and he came to me ... but why it wasn't working? I never got any answers. Instead I got more love; I met more people, and more fell in love with me, while my nickname became runaway mist. I became like a mist, meeting today, enjoying my time, and blocking them on every network and communication way possible. My block list outnumbered my friends' list; was it revenge, was my trust in men diminishing by the minute, and by every encounter, or was it the fear of men's reaction at the end of the day? Where was I heading? What were my plans? All I know, there were honest people out there, but I couldn't believe in their honesty. Are you for real, are you staying, are you ready to commit, and why do you love me? Questions that should never be there when discussing love, but I could not see the honesty in men, their words and their intentions. To me, men became a ball of lies, and personal interests. I'm sure along the way I lost or will lose the one and only, honest person but, I couldn't let myself go beyond the cup of coffee to see and feel the truth.

Talking about the tall, short, handsome, big, small, blue eyes, green eyes, bold, hairy, etc. ... along the way, I met them all, but all I saw was dishonesty; and I planned my runaway, before going to meet them. Sad, but true, and the only truth was that I was alone, sharing stories with myself, and convincing myself that men were all the same, and were with me for a reason.

Christmas was close, I decided to celebrate, and take my life to the next level against all odds. I had taken the breast cancer exam earlier in June 2013, and the gynecologist had asked me to repeat the tests in six months, fearing some symptoms in the exam. I couldn't celebrate with the issue on my mind, I contacted the hospital, took an appointment and decided to face the results, as they came, before the holidays. The appointment was on the twenty-first December 2013, and to my luck, there were no developments and all was negative. I was thrilled, at least to that news, but still heartbroken. Yet, the Christmas tree was up and spirit of Christmas was stronger. On the twenty-third December 2013, I parked my car, and as I was crossing the street to go home, between a daydream and a dream, I stopped in the middle of the street and got run over by a car. I flew in the air, my purse, its contents and the laptop scattered on the street. I was laying down flat on my back, for seconds that lasted forever, among the screaming of people on the street and the noise from the breaks of all the cars passing, my life flashed in front of my eyes. I couldn't tell whether I was alive or dead, but with the will of life, and Christmas, I heard my daughters calling, I stood on my feet, collected my things off the ground, looked at all the crowd, and with a smile on my face, and numbness in my brain and body, I walked home. It was at that moment that I decided to enjoy my life, family and myself again.

Till the next call to jump, young love stayed around, he never left, which made my questions more complicated, why did he want me, and was he for real?

The next summer, I woke up one day, to see the box where I locked the ghosts of my past open and the lock was broken. The past woke up, the ghosts regenerated their energy, called for assistance, and came back. At first, I did not know their plan, but it did not take long for change to take place. They stirred the mud and wrecked the bridges of my new journey and era; they extracted my dreams from their roots and left me with nothing. Conflicts happened, again, but this time more serious than any prior time, I became jobless, family-less, and back alone, worried about my future, well-being and the future of my daughters.

I was lost, distorted, depressed, scared, uncertain of my potential, and at my lowest point ever. Am I a loser, in love and in person, because that is how I felt! I couldn't see my strength, or even remember my achievements; I couldn't think straight, to enable myself to stand again; where did everything go? Was I in a dream? I surely hoped so … but in reality, I was not. I informed my ex-husband of my current situation, and I tried to move on. I guess, with time, and at a specific age, moving on becomes truly heavy, and especially, that this time, it was not moving on a specific task, it was a new start up. I could not launch again, at least not again, not now, and not as quickly as I should.

I contacted an old best friend of mine, a friend I called Winter, a friend that truly knew the meaning of friendship, and with no second thoughts, he offered the help needed, from emotional to financial, and at least without asking for anything in return. Friends like him are rare to find, we barely encounter one in our lifetime, and that, only if we are lucky enough. This guy, since my adolescence, was there; I guess he was my guardian angel; he stood by me throughout, I stood by him regardless and against all odds; he was the real savior and I was the true friend. He shows up out of nowhere, he holds my hand, cares for my wounds, and dries my tears; he understands my pain without talking; he takes care of things and once I'm ready, he leaves without goodbyes. To him, I am strong enough to handle any misery, therefore, he leaves me when he sees I'm ready. But this time, he couldn't leave, so he stayed near, he was worried, he knew that this time the fall was tough, hurtful, and painful. He sat there, watched me cry, he wiped my tears with his own hands, and even worse, he cried with me. He cried not to show his support, but because this was the first time he saw how helpless I was. Although he believed in me, my potential and my strength, he knew, as well, that a vacation was due. He took care of everything, and asked me to rest, and take a vacation. Anyways, I couldn't do more.

It is funny how humans function, at one point they can handle the world, and suddenly, they lose every muscle and brain to stand again. That is where I was, a vegetable watering myself with my own tears.

Chapter 18

With all the mess around me, my disastrous financial situation, and my emotional crash, I couldn't but think about fairytale love. I know, you are probably saying, how could I be thinking about love in a time like this, but I always believed that love can change the world. Love steers people's life, from bad to good; love makes people feel better, both those who love passionately things and people, and those who receive passionate love; and last, love is the essence of life and can bring a dead body to life.

Heart to heart confession, I was longing for fairytale love … probably because I was weak and needed his passion, but I believe it's all about the way he looked at me, and made me feel without him touching me; it's how I felt when he was not around, the emptiness, loneliness, heartache to see him, be with him, touch him; it's how much I wanted to hear his voice, to chat with him, and laugh; it's about the feeling of joy, happiness, and ecstasy, when I closed my eyes and thought of him. It's about the times I feel his gentle lips on my forehead, and how I start shivering; it's about the times I felt his kisses scrolling down my ears, and all over my body; it's about the sensational feeling when our shadows touch, and how our blood boils inside our veins; it was, fairytale love and me.

Did you ever feel this way? Did love ever change you? Did you ever meet your fairytale love?

Did you ever hear someone talking to you when he was away?

Did you ever feel someone touching you when he is not around you?

Did you ever imagine someone whispering in your ears when he's not there?

Did you ever miss someone's love after he was gone?

Well, what makes you love someone so much? And do you believe in love?

Many would say, no, I do not believe in true love, it does not exist. Partially it is their ego taking part in the conversation, but who does not need love, and to be loved? Is that why people live love in their dreams ... more than in reality?

Why is it that, us women, enjoy the passionate love in a book? The more erotic it is, the more we don't let go of. Is it because we live it, we long for those moments? When watching a movie, we imagine ourselves emotionally involved, we even go to the extent of living the passionate scenes, we feel them, and in our heart, we wish them happening to us. When we watch a romantic action, we wish it happened to us. From simple breakfast in bed, to a flower with an invitation card for dinner on the pillow, to a head to head wine and cheese dinner, to a movie, to dedicating a song in a text message. Why is it that some of us imagine being with another woman and wonder how it feels? Or fantasize about the feeling of being touched by someone other than our partner? Why is it that we enjoy watching a movie secretly, in our bedroom, be it simple acts or the erotic side? Why is it that we tend to chat with other men and/or women, and release our dreams, fantasies, and simple conversations away from our partners? Are we longing for attention, are we not satisfied with our partner? Is he not fulfilling our dream? Are we not living the fantasy moment with him? Do we feel intimidated exploring our bodies? Do we fear being judged? Do we believe our intimate moments are duties rather than desire? Did our intimate time become purely the need for it and not the dream and longing to be with that person or our partner? Are we ignoring our needs? Do we not dare to ask for what we love when intimate? Are we intimidated to ask for a specific touch? Does a massage by a stranger give us more lust than being touched by our partner? Does intimacy mean anything to us? Or were we never with any other partner and therefore we do not know what is out there? Then why do we share those moments with our best friend, whether verbally, or go the full way in talks and actions? Why is it that we live more desires when our shadows collide with a stranger, we feel emotional bursts? Why is it that we feel a joy when receiving a compliment from strangers? Why is it that we accept to be the woman leaving from the back door while we can and deserve to be someone's queen and use the main door?

Dear colleagues in the emotional field, love is the essence of life. It is the blood that pumps through your heart to keep it young and alive. Ignoring that essence will result in a dry bed, and soon after, two beds. Be the shy woman on the streets and sexy in the sheets. Be the women on top, be the leader in action, in asking, in wanting, in the desire. Let your man know your demands, your need, and your fantasies. Dare to be the one asking, and not have enough. Keep your partner under your spell. Keep him admiring your imagination, inform yourself, inquire, and research. Let him wonder, why you look beautiful today, why your eyes are sparkling? Let him go to work satisfied, and looking forward to come back home, for you. Let him miss you, let him remember you when not around. Careful, do not burden him, do not live a routine, or set schedules. Be innovative, be creative, and consider him your child's art project. Put an effort in your bed, and dare to touch him where no one ever did and will. Your sheets are the secret of your passion, they should never be neat. Let him wonder about the source of change, let him see the change in different outfits, hairstyle, lipstick and perfume. Keep the candles lit, and make sure the flame keeps on burning. Add music, use oil, whisper in his ears, and let him feel your breathing when you are not around. Occasionally, change the setup, and dare to be the other woman, be the woman he fantasizes about. It is your right to be loved, to receive what you want, to be treated the way you like, and to be touched the way you desire. No task should have a priority over your love, desires and intimate moments.

Be a star in your own eyes before someone else's eyes. If you chose to be a housewife, don't sink in your children's life and ignore yourself. Yourself, means your unity with your partner. Remember that children are passing in our life and moving on to their own path, and once they do, you do not want to end up with a dry bed. Your duty towards your children is timeless, precious and treasurable. But remember, it should be measurable, for you as a unity with your husband, and for them. Create independent humans, for them before being for you, and keep in mind that you are their model, in love, in life, and in actions. Your children will appreciate you whatever you do for them, but be the woman they challenge themselves to be or have as life partners. So if you chose to be a housewife, involve yourself in community work. Have a novelty to discuss with your partner, be interactive, set standards for yourself, and work to meet them. Keep your day busy, between the house, children, and little tasks, and don't end up waiting for your partner to keep entertaining you. Your heart is a magic wand, and your mind is a dormant creative hub, don't be the woman waiting for change to come knock at her door, there is plenty of volunteer work, on a part time basis, waiting for your care. Go out, explore the world, and reach new potential. Believe in yourself, no one no matter how much they appreciate you, will do that for you. Many men might prefer to know that their woman is secure at home. They might want that, and being the devil's advocate, I will say it's out of care, thinking they provide all household needs, and wanting you to rest and enjoy your life. But other men might do it out of a selfish point of view, in order to worry less. Some men are intimidated by their partner's success, and therefore, this would lead to intimidation in the sheets. Play it smart, handle them with care, and develop their fragile side. Remember that a magic wand in a hand, is a transformation in a life. And it is your life, your heart, your emotions, and your desires.

If you chose to be an outgoing woman, and whether you are that outgoing woman, or you suddenly felt the need for change, keep in mind that men don't accept or adapt to change as fast as we do. Firstly, equality to most of them, is a vocabulary in the dictionary, more than in reality, although they may claim to believe in equality. Your job may require a social skill, and a social involvement, that would make them feel inferior. Men transmute their emotions to the sheets, therefore many want to be on top, and lead. Perception is a major factor in reality, therefore, letting them hold the wheel, does not mean they steer the relationship in the direction they want. The secret lies in your hand, and a smart woman is the one that makes her partner feel and believe he is the master of destiny, without him knowing that she plays a major role being the pillow whisperer. He might be the king of the jungle, but who lives there? The blood flows to the heart, and the heart of the house is you, the woman first, and then out to the world. So handle him, manipulate your destiny, and make him believe he is the one behind your success. Who knows, you might end up with the only special man that admires women's success, and especially if she is his partner. Life is a puzzle, and it is put together by humans. The reason behind calling it a puzzle, is for people to assemble it their own way, and based on their field of vision towards it. Some may start by the corners, some on the sides, and others start in the heart. The pieces represent the different components of your life, and the steps are your priority. At the end, all will reach the same picture, your life, your love life, your job. The colors are your emotions. We all have one picture, and one picture in mind, but the way to put it together differs among our personalities. Don't let your puzzle end up colorless, transparent, or in black and white. Shades of colors are the ups and downs of our life, they resemble the emotions we go through to make it complete. Dull colors are the monotony that leave us uninterested; lively colors are the beautiful moments; highlighted colors are the intense passionate moments; and mixed colors are the changing cycles. Change is to represent continuity. Those who do not care about change shall never develop their relationship, because we no longer think the way we did when we met, we no longer love the way we did when we met, and mainly, our dream changed, we have changed, and we are no longer the couple we were when we met. Let your inside dare to change with your outside, live the passion you desire, live it with your partner, face him, and change him with you. We are no longer the couple that originally met, not physically, emotionally or mentally. Women are the leaders in emotions. You may choose to accept your partner's negligence and indifference towards you; but remember that you hold the magic wand. Men do not know how much you want until they hear it, they do not know what you desire until you give those signs and hints. Your experience develops with age, and that will happen after experiencing each other and knowing pleasurable moments together. Enjoying each other as a couple should remain on the top of the list. Love yourself before requesting your partner's love, you are the image of his success; shine and let him see you sparkling. Men consider their women and then their families, their commodities; they take pride in their happiness, success, etc. … because they consider us among their achievements, no matter how sweet they are.

Dear colleagues in the emotional battlefield, time is on our side, with time we change physically, but intimately we learn to reach ultimate pleasures. Some feel that age means the deterioration of the body; but as women change physically, men go through the same concerns; you are not alone, mid-life crisis is not just a general statement. Don't fail to live your passion, to love passionately, and be loved passionately. I failed to win my battle, to set my cards open on the table, and to impose my needs; I ended up walking my journey in parallel with my partner, and living my passionate dream elsewhere.

Should I regret the outcome? Are all men alike, and are all women alike? The answer remains in the mind of the reader, as we will never know what a passionate relationship is till we undress totally, physically and emotionally. That passionate love strikes occasionally, and we encounter it only when we let go in the arms of the only one offering us unconditional love, lust, and passion; and I was lucky to find mine!

Chapter 19

Whether in dream or reality, everyone is seeking love. Relationships are an adventure, and their success is related to how much we offer, dare to give, and we challenge ourselves to maintain. It is similar to any personal business or job task. We are excited to launch, we find different mechanisms to overcome the hurdles, we manage the difficulty wisely, and we take pride in its long-term stability. Relationships are an achievement, and the main achievement we should focus on. Men take in their own achievements, they work hard to survive, but why do they reach a point of ignoring at times, and it's a general statement, the inside of their own home. No one wants to end what they started; our goal in any relationship is continuity, but many times we fail. Failure is a lack of interest, motivation, as it takes one person to start a task, but it's the responsibility of two to survive.

Dear men, in the course of life, do you know what you want? Do you know your priorities and what makes you happy? Do you ever wonder where you failed? I will answer you from a woman's perspective, because I lived the deception, and I believe that it is a mutual effort. A relationship is conceived between Adam and Eve, the day they meet. They see the apple that will bring them together, but they forget the tree. Once we take the first bite, we focus on the rest of the apple, but we tend to ignore why we took the first bite, and what happens after we finish it. We forget that the apple has seeds, and they are meant to be re-planted deep down in our souls to replenish. We cut the apple in half, we see the star inside each one of us, but then if we leave it open and don't eat it all, it will dry. Apples are meant to be devoured, like love, they are meant to be enjoyed, and mainly, we should never forget why we first wanted that apple, and the taste of the first bite.

Men draw their path, and plan their life. They live their crazy days with pleasure, and most of them, want to have an apple tree. They are the roots, and women are the trunk of the tree; branches and leaves are their life together. No man wants to have only the roots, but why is it that they ignore watering the tree of life? What women want is simple: happiness. We want you to be the man every other woman envies, we want you to be our security, and our continuity. We want our man to be the reason for our smile, and the man in our dreams. Although we find happiness in a stranger's look, compliment or admiration, when it comes from our man, we find contentment. A compliment about the meal we cooked, the dress, the nightgown etc. ... can keep us in assertiveness that you are ours. We don't like sharing you, but the jealousy we reach when another woman looks at you, or envies us in having you is a sign of love and not lack of trust. Don't let us reach a point of careless reaction; don't let us reach a point of ignoring each other. You are the smile of reassurance that we are in good hands, you are the shoulder on which we lay our head for support, and you are the listening ear of our emotions. We do not want to seek understanding elsewhere, we need to know that you are here for us, and you take pleasure in our love. You may or may not have promised us that rainbow in rainy days, but surely, you are the treasure at the end. We, women, are blessed with patience, we are blessed with unconditional giving power, but we need to feel the mutual giving. We need to see the extra mile you cross for us, in order to walk the extra miles for you. Romance is a key term for us, so be that romantic giver, be the man carrying the rose occasionally. Don't underestimate us, many men out there can find the woman inside us and appreciate the beauty of our soul, but we prefer your attention. You are the one we based our dream on the day we ate that apple, and said "I do," so take charge of your "I do," and remember the dream we meant to build together. Don't force the negligence into our actions, don't lead us to indifference, and don't let us reach a point of duty towards each other; because the day we close the door behind us, it will be difficult to reopen it again.

Did you ever wonder what women want? It's a general statement, but basically, women are simply looking for memories.

No matter what we build together, or what we lose together, our memories together are what keep things on the right track. Close your eyes, go back in time, and try to remember, how many times did your partner say, "Honey, do you remember ..." This is us! We are the photos, a memory box, and a hub for the events and the feelings we had at that time. You would know the kind of woman we are, from the way we deal with our children. But we don't want to be only that woman in your eyes, we want to be the other woman.

Could a couple, man and a woman, be the be-all and end-all for each other? Yes, though it requires a wide maturity, know-how, and wisdom on behalf of the woman, and yet, it is always a general statement.

Men overall, need to feel trusted. Following a man, tracking his activities, and doubting what he says, could only result in a hesitant life; and the same applies to the woman. Except, men in general, need a time alone, away from duties and concern. Some may only enjoy a card game, while others may go a step further to seek what they miss at home, the special care.

Men need to know their woman is waiting for them, if this is happening, great.

Men need to know their woman knows their favorite meal, if this is happening, great.

Men need to be caressed on the hair, neck, and shoulder, when you pass by them in public, it makes them feel royal.

Men need to feel we want them when they approach us intimately. Men start the communication in bed, while women are attracted to bed through the conversation.

Men prefer to hear the short version of the story, than to hear the details, men are characterized by a short span attention; therefore, to make things easier and avoid a reason for conflict, start the story with its purpose, such as, honey, I need your opinion, your help, listen to what I did, etc. ...

Men need to feel needed, they love to solve your problems; but make sure it happens occasionally, and show your appreciation in public.

Men need to feel they are the source of comfort and happiness to the family.

Men need to feel they are satisfying you, intimately. As there is always a leader on house tasks level, there is always a leader in the sheets, and it may not be the same person. Especially don't let your man feel you are the leader in the sheets, but be innovative, and get out of your way, to say and do things differently.

Men need to know they can trust the woman at home, in terms of all responsibilities, and in terms of standing for herself when outside.

Men need to be heard, so pay attention.
Men need to be listened to, so communicate.
Men need to be loved, so open up.
Men need to be touched, so give them that satisfaction.
Men need to be appreciated, so show them that care.
Men need to feel that you won't let go easily, so hold on tight.
Men need passion, so don't shy away.
Men need one woman, so be that woman.

But wait, don't we all, and aren't we all looking for that extra care, love, and passion? Both men and women, go through mid-life crises, and both will end up opening a window for a new breeze, and fresh air if their needs are not met and satisfied. What applies to one, applies to the other, and what is allowed for one, is allowed for the other. If men need all these mentioned above, so do women. Success in unity is the product of both efforts; leaving issues unresolved will result in letting go of each other; there is a beginning to all conflicts, there is a missing link in every misunderstanding, and surely, somewhere along the common road, one of the couple involved lost interest in continuity. There is always a reason for things to change, and a feeder for that reason. Both of us have changed, and we both react differently now; our priorities are still the same, but as time goes by, we start wondering about the years left for us. It is the nature of the beast, wanting it all. Early in life, we needed time to get used to each other, we needed time to understand every look and unspoken word, and additionally, adapt to each other's character, while maintaining our own. Everything is new, and shortly after, children pop up, his family, my family, friends ... we tend to forget ourselves, slowly ignore personal needs and interests, and we forget that passion is the key to our long-term serenity.

When small conflicts, issues, misunderstandings, and disagreements, go out of proportion, it's a call for the couple to stop, rewind, and replay. Neglecting interventions will lead to a gap between the couple, and soon after to profound disturbed emotions. Do you know why? And I'm directing my question to you, sir, my partner, my man, the love of my life, my honey, my sugar, my soulmate, my best friend ... and add on to that many more titles. Do you know why we became distant? Do you remember why? Do you remember when? Do you care to know why? Did you stop caring?

How do we know that our partner is changing? Well, at times we all need an exit, a breakthrough, and when this time comes, the role of the partner is crucial. Letting go, judging, or making them accountable for their actions is not the solution. If you know your partner well, you will notice the changes. So, get to know your partner, their needs, their moods, and their unspoken words; read their body language, facial expressions, loss of interest, change of habits, etc. ... Many symptoms are the call for alert, in addition to many other points like a change of schedule, loss of appetite, weight loss or gain, change of style ...

But why does our partner change? Is it because the routine took over; we both sunk taking care of the family; we stopped caring for our personal needs; we forgot to arrange personal time; we found easier pleasure elsewhere, in a room away from personal stress; we turned off the candle of lust; we pursued passionate time away from home because we felt intimidated by our fantasies; we saw the physical changes in our partner; we are no longer attracted to each other; one of us lost interest in intimacy; we failed to relay our desires; we put our ego before our relationship; we did way more; are those the reasons behind our differences? Partially yes, but mainly we hurt each other up to a point where we did not care enough to look back, and come back.

At times of conflict between the couple, the blame falls on both. Mistakes happen by both parties, and rarely a third party does the right thing bringing them back closer and together. I agree that marriage should last forever, but when it becomes a torture to either one, and one of the couple is not willing to subdue and meet halfway for the sake of the other partner, a solution must take place, and sadly, many times the solution results in the termination of the relationship.

There are always possibilities, there are many ways to conciliate, but only if there is a will, and yet, many times it may not succeed.

Although I divorced after twenty years of marriage, I still believe that having a partner is very important in life. It is important to know that someone is waiting to end the day with me, and this someone is the first one I want to see in the morning. Keep your unity as a priority, keep the candle of love lit, keep a rose in the back of the car, keep the champagne bubbling, and always keep your partner as your first priority.

Our happiness is our sanity, if it does not work with one, it will work with another.

Dear partner of ours, we urge you not to let go easily, we urge you to remember the memories we built together, because if you don't, someone else will take over, and in their turn, they will be our happiness and sanity.

Chapter 20 ... And a new era begins!

Today, I am about to commemorate my first fifty, and all I can say, what a life!

I am sitting in a coffee shop, and thinking about my life. There are people sitting here and there, and at a table behind me a group of middle-aged women are talking, and I couldn't help but hear their conversation. The same conversation I hear on a daily basis; couples splitting, women divorcing, their husbands not coping with the marriage, sleeping in two separate rooms, sharing financial house duties, and living as partners. That is the story of every house, sadly, but a true statement; is marriage becoming a disappointment!

On another table, a couple that met online, also middle-aged, meaning they either did not make it through their marriage, or did not find their match yet.

Way inside, in the corner, a man and a woman also middle-aged, both wearing their wedding bands, meaning, either, a married couple, or sneaking a relationship out, and most likely, this is the situation. He is caressing her hand, feeding her, and undressing her with his eyes; her legs are crossed, and she is touching him under the table. I know the couple, they are not each other's half officially, they complete each other's contentment.

In the middle of the lounge, a party of ten, early twenties, celebrating a birthday. I'm looking at them, happy, and full of life; and I said to myself, I remember those days. I wonder how long it will last, and I wonder whether they know what is awaiting them in the future.

Marriage, to me, is a must, but is the society reflecting its success to the younger generation, and do I reflect it to my own daughters? Did my success in life stand in the way of my family? Are working women becoming a threat to society, and men in general? Or are there men out there, who still believe in equality, and are not intimidated by successful women? Well, I did raise my daughters to take charge of their lives, and I truly hope this was not a mistake. But in view of my life, and the life of the women around me, I believed it was the right thing to do.

Life is a journey, and a journey worth taking. We are passing through, and the day we debark to eternity, all we take with us is the joyful moments we lived. Unfortunately, the rules of life do not come in a standardized format, and our days were based on the choices we took throughout. There are no rewind systems, to edit events, nor is there a replay mode; all there is, refresh old self and move on.

A recap to who I am today, in the eyes of a fifty-year-old woman. I wish I knew in the past what I know today, but, in every phase, I thought I dealt with every situation with advanced and upgraded maturity. I am a woman built from cement. I proved it to myself, and to my surroundings. I never accepted failure; I used the pebbles I tripped on across my path to build my own castle from scratch. I love old music, and ballroom dancing, but I never was the old school type, instead I conquered the world with an open mind and challenged myself to embark following my own feelings and instinct. I have always shown impulsiveness with my decisions, and took responsibility for my actions. I enjoy food, I am a social drinker, I love to smoke cigars, and Mediterranean hookah, and to me, those who enjoy food, music, and the dance floor, they appreciate life. I do appreciate life, I take the best out of every situation, and I believe that things happen for a reason. I am very superstitious, I believe in the power of the universe, and I believe that we are born with an aura that determines our personality. My aura was positivity, and it was the driving force of my life. I believe in the power of the smile, and laughter, and I believe that nothing is worth shedding tears for; yet, I am very sensitive, and emotional. I am intrinsically motivated, and I am lucky to possess an inner strength for continuity. Equality between men and women runs through my veins, and rarely can a man achieve what women cannot. I always felt blessed, and until today, and regardless of all the fortunate and unfortunate events in my life, I still feel new successes are awaiting me out there. I am passionate about life, and all its content, from things to living creatures. I just love life, enjoy every moment, and cherish every situation. As well, I see relationships as a vicious circle I can't keep up with, but surely can't stay without. Love shadowed me throughout my journey; closing one door always opened many; I always gave more than I received, but after trust in men was jeopardized, I started giving with limitations.

Men and me, I became a shooting star, appearing to them, and enjoying the running away. I intended the exit, planned it, and never looked back. I felt no one was worth my trust, and I found a loophole in each situation. I started believing they are not meant to be, knowing, most likely along the way, I would lose the one worth connecting with. My "ex-husband" was a partner, I was driven by passion, and passion was not there. I exited after twenty years for freedom; "soulmate" was the one that spread the bed of roses after my divorce, he couldn't commit to his promises of letting go of his country, and to be honest, I preferred not to be the reason behind his detachment. I wanted someone who would love me enough to break through from his roots without hesitation. "Old love" was just a fantasy to me, he was the one I loved passionately before my marriage, he was the one I wondered about throughout my years of marriage, and the one who deceived me on every level, including financial, after my divorce, yet I do believe he loved me. "Young soul" was the encounter of passionate love and lust, yet, his age was the wall that is still standing in the way of what could be eternity. "Shadow soul" was the young love I loved at a pure age, when he shocked me with his appearance along with another lady, on my seventeenth birthday, but he proved to be a good friend. "Angel love" was the one I lost in a terrorist attack.

Can you see the pattern? I tell you, today I believe, so far, no relationship was meant to last, with a message, nothing lasts forever. So between those that let go of me, and those that had excuses to let go, I lost faith in men. I feared connecting, and planned the run away, with every next one I encountered. My intentions became the one night stand, with no looking back.

As for the ghosts of the past, I am positive you are still wondering about who they were. Let me tell you, after my journey with them, and them popping out to destroy my life successively, I stopped believing they were there to hurt me, instead I started believing that they were the reason behind my success. I believe inside each one of us, there is a ghost, a ghost that rebels on our emotions and tries to wreck the happiness of others, but as well I affirm that our ghosts shall come back and hunt us, to defeat us and stand in the way of our own happiness; our ghosts are the karma of our actions. So everyone who sent their ghost my way, their ghost shadowed them with guilt, loneliness and disappointments. Dear ghost of the past, you did not break me, instead, you made me stronger, you made me realize that things happen for a reason, every time you blocked a path for me, a stronger holy power opened many options for me. I may not have chosen the everlasting happiness with either choice I made, but I surely found love, success, and serenity in my choices. No, I never regretted any path I chose to follow, because in each, I discovered more success. No regret was one of my mottos, and if evaluating my life today, I don't think anyone, married, single, or separated, has been loved and still is passionately encountering lust and passion, as much as I ever did, am, and still will.

I am blessed with two beautiful and successful daughters, I see my success and blessings in them. Today I am fifty years old, I will be closing this chapter of my life. Let me tell you, I don't know how a fifty-year-old woman should feel, but I do feel great, I don't feel halfway through, instead I feel I have not started living yet, and the best is yet to come.

I am bixxy – big and sexy – I am a beautiful woman, I don't feel fifty or look fifty. I have true friends despite all I went through, we exchange true memories; I lived more passion than one can handle in a lifetime, and I exchanged true relationships, more than a single person can ever have; and I have a beautiful family; I may not have the classical one, but the one I have is unique. I lived around the world, and travelled more than anyone else did, just because I always felt that the world was within my reach. I was saluted by both men and women, for my guts, and I am a woman who walked her path tall, and was proud of her achievements. What else could a woman desire? Yes, I did shed many tears, but I always had someone wiping them for me, supporting my back, escorting me during my downs, and happy for me during my ups. Although today, I do not have someone in charge or in partnership of my life, a full-timer but it is just because I did not decide to let go, and trust fully. I enjoy my own company when I choose to be alone, but I am surrounded by beautiful people if I decide to be accompanied. Winter, eclipse, fairytale love, etc. … are all there for me, they are my true friends, passionate men, soulmates, and everything to me. Life is a journey, worth the ups and downs, especially, when we consider it worthy of all incidents. No one lives a steady happiness, for a very simple reason, we cannot appreciate what we have, till we earn it, we cannot earn happiness till we shed tears, and tears of happiness are the results of tears of sorrow.

My birth mother was taken away from me at birth, I never met her, she never even held me in her arms, but the angel that stood silent in the corner, in the birth room where it all started, was her soul, which escorted me, and gave me power, blessings, and guidance from above throughout my life. I believe my birth mother was my guardian angel, and she was the one that shook me to hold on to life, when I froze in front of the car that hit me December 23, 2013. It is tough for someone to still see the positive if they lived a life like mine, but I now believe that my life was, and still is, a journey worth taking.

If I am given a second chance, would I make the same choices? I would only add to meet my birth mother, view all I heard about her; and yet, if given a choice to change the whole thing, or take it as is, I will take it as is. Living and regretting is better than regretting to live, and I lived my life, not regretting a moment, because I never failed to enjoy the moment as it was offered. I did the best I could, with the best way I know of, and the results so far are satisfying. I was born with a rebel soul, I was blessed with continuity, I was given an agile character, I was set with a short term memory to pain, and therefore, I was able to survive.

I wish life came with a handbook, even though, unless you are a standard soul living by the book, the handbook cannot help you. Personally, I made my own handbook, I lived by it, updated it as needed, and put the rules of life after I had lived the different scenarios. I discovered there aren't two similar circumstances that were solved identically. I always believed that situations are viewed differently depending on the eyes of the viewer, and the same situations are perceived differently by the same person, depending on the age, emotional status, and maturity of that individual at that time.

Watch for painful memories and pain, don't let them hold you back. Should we forgive, forget, or isolate what hurt us to protect ourselves? I believe, painful memories are buried deep inside, and ready to emerge at the earliest similar situation to intensify the current pain. As for forgiveness … it's an added word to the dictionary. Forgiveness is an action towards others, it is centered on emotions, and it will not heal you. Additionally, you cannot forgive others because the minute actions repeat themselves, you will relate the incidents, in your mind and out loud. As for forgetfulness, it is centered on the mind, it is a firewall, and time taught me not to forget fully. Forgetting others' actions towards you, will only encourage others to repeat their actions. Forgetting is a self-protection mechanism created by each of us individuals, we build it to hide behind it. As I result, I believe, in times of distress, I should not be the prosecutor, and I shall never be the devil's advocate. People always have justifications for their actions, therefore, discussing with others that they were hurtful is a lose-lose situation. People react differently. Some believe that if you don't create an issue from hurtful situations, you become an open target to successive pain; I believe, the shorter the quarrel is, the healthier it becomes, after all, one of the secret of success is to keep others wondering about the time you will revolt, and additionally, I prefer to start the healing process, and use the pain as exit steps towards a safe land, before I end up isolating it. It is good to discuss issues on the spot, but be smart not to sink in a pattern of back and forth, endless communications that will lead you nowhere. An important thing in life, get to know the people or person you are dealing with, and more importantly, protect yourself. In general, people are self-centered, and rarely might they put other's priorities before their own, they don't care about anyone beyond their four walls. They may help you, advise you, check on you occasionally, but the main source of power that will pull you up again, is inside you. Cry all you want, but remember to float on your tears. Every tear you shed is a step towards healing; analyze it, and understand its content; and develop it to build your strength on it. If you forget the pain and its source, it will come back to hurt you again. It you forgive those who hurt you, it might be used as a weakness.

So, if you decide to forgive, you do it because you are a nice person, and not because those who hurt you deserve a second chance, and I am not saying people do not deserve a second chance; if you decide to forget, it is because you should not sink in others' hurtful game, you should forget and rather ignore, in order to heal yourself; after all, it's the situations we live and survive that make us stronger, wiser, and more agile. All I am saying, those who hurt you, are not worth your time. Your well-being comes first, and all the strength you need to stand alone is within you. It is important to lean on others, but more importantly, it is important to know you have people you can lean on. Those people are genuine and rare to encounter, but they are there. Each will provide a different support, but the combination will do.

Many people made a difference in my life, and some didn't even know it. I believe we meet people for a reason, our paths cross with a message, and one day or another, we will know why. Many people who were in my life when I was young, disappeared, and came back into my life oddly; and others that were there when I was born, disappeared forever, I never knew they existed, they found me, and we mysteriously reconnected. Despite the distance, they became closer to me than anyone I see on daily basis.

What they don't know, they came in a time when I was in need of them or will be in need of them. That is why I cherish what I have, and whom I have in my life. I believe everyone in our life is a jewel; some are fake, others are semi-precious, and there are those who are rare and pure. That is why I never ask anyone to go out of my life, there is a place for everyone, and those who are no longer here, have chosen the way out themselves.

The future was always part of my thoughts; I always feared to plan it, but never failed to dream about it. My dreams never stood in the way of my happiness, despite the changes that happened. But in all situations, my main concern was the end. May I ask you how are you planning the end? It's very simple, before you know it, age strikes your door year after year. Today, you may tell yourself, it is ok to sacrifice my time and life for others, but shortly you will find yourself alone. Take every chance, embrace every opportunity, and embark on every dream; live with love, and love with passion; attract life like a magnet and let the universe follow your shadow; you don't need to fly in order to have your head in the clouds, dare to let go, live freely within your surroundings, and, enjoy life.

As for me and love, I believe I have encountered love and passion more than any human being ever did. Regardless of the trust issue that stood between me and men, I was blessed to be loved, cherished, and treated passionately.

I am sure you are wondering where I would land? Well, I have the options on the table, and for now, I would rather keep it up to you to choose for me.

If life is about privileges, I should go with …
If life is about money, I should go with …
If life is about family, I should go with …
If life is about passion, I should go with …
If life is about love, I should go with …
Do you know what life is all about?
Do you know what men or women would want after years together, from the men or women they linked to, years ago?
Do you know what you want in the future?

Can you ever go back in time?

Well, if you don't have all the answers, you cannot plan your life, and especially not plan and control your feelings and emotions. Tomorrow is far from being planned, and once you hit the day you are living, you are way behind on planning. Life is made of laughter and pain cells, and emotions are contagious and reproducible. Laugh out loud, and bring the smile into your surroundings; cry, it's ok to cry if needed, but not ok to sink. So stay beautiful, walk tall, and enjoy every mistake, as this is what makes you the woman you are today.

Chapter 21

Once upon a time, a child was born. Between the different events, that child learned that the end in sight is more important than the beginning. My story is not unique, maybe the sequence happening to one person is. I am every woman, every story behind closed doors, every marriage, and every company.

I want to thank my male friends for speaking out, telling me about their fear, discussing their concerns, and making things clear to me.

Your life is the shadow that escorts you day in and day out. When your shadow struggles with you wanting to split or go in different directions, it's your soul wanting to live and remain alive. Whatever you do, do it for you, you deserve to live your destiny.

Here it was, in a world full of adventures and people, I lived my own life, differently from any standard written, or once told. I learned to survive with the enemy, understand the opponent, play others' games, but master my own.

Today I learned that life is a game, and from now on, I will play only the parts I want.

Today I know that winning or succeeding is mostly important in the eyes of the bearer.

Today, I still believe that family is very important, but I understand that not all families are identical; I am also convinced that men and women are best soulmates.

Today, I tell you, anytime throughout your life, you can start. The beginning is set to the time you reset your heart and mind to take charge of the body and soul, and give them what they want. There is no rule that says when things must start by, or a law that you must complete your task by.

Once upon a time, a child was born, that child was a baby girl, that girl started growing, she became a woman, a wife and a mother, she learned many things, but mainly she learned that life is precious, time flies faster that the clock ticking, and that life is all about finding self and not proving it to others.

       With Every New Day, A New Beginning ...

Rate this book on our website!

www.novum-publishing.co.uk

The author

Badiaa Hiresh was born in Lebanon in 1964 where she eventually lived and worked, raising two daughters. Badiaa also spent time in the USA which gives her a unique international perspective on her home country. After working as an accountant and manager for the family jewelry business, Badiaa found herself in the field of education, helping to start a school. As well as writing, Badiaa is an advocate for peace, spending many years as a Peace Coordinator.

novum 👍 PUBLISHER FOR NEW AUTHORS

The publisher

„ **Whoever stops getting better, will in time stop being good.**

This is the motto of novum publishing, and our focus is on finding new manuscripts, publishing them and offering long-term support to the authors.
Our publishing house was founded in 1997, and since then it has become THE expert for new authors and has won numerous awards.

Our editorial team will peruse each manuscript within a few weeks free of charge and without obligation.

You will find more information about
novum publishing and our books on the internet:

w w w . n o v u m - p u b l i s h i n g . c o . u k